D1121735

THE REAL STORIES OF HOCKEY NIGHT IN CANADA

WALKING with LEGENDS

Ralph Mellanby

with Mike Brophy

Foreword by Don Cherry

FENN

Fenn Publishing Company Ltd.

Bolton, Ontario

Fenn Publishing Company Ltd.

WALKING WITH LEGENDS
A Fenn Publishing Book / First Published in 2007

Fenn Publishing Company Ltd.
Bolton, Ontario, Canada
www.hbfenn.com

The publisher gratefully acknowledges the support of the Canada Council for the Arts and the
Ontario Arts Council for its publishing program. We acknowledge the support of the Government
of Ontario through the Ontario Media Development Corporation's Ontario Book Initiative.

We acknowledge the financial support of the Government of Canada through the Book Publishing
Industry Development Program (BPIDP) for our publishing activities. Care has been taken to trace
ownership of copyright material in this book and to secure permissions. The publishers will gladly
receive any information that will enable them to rectify errors or omissions.

Text design: Laura Brunton

Printed and bound in Canada

Library and Archives Canada Cataloguing in Publication

Mellanby, Ralph
    **Walking with legends : the real stories of hockey night in canada / Ralph Mellanby with Mike
Brophy ; Don Cherry, prologue.**

ISBN 978-1-55168-305-8

    1. Mellanby, Ralph. 2. National Hockey League–Biography.
3. Hockey–Biography. 4. Hockey night in Canada (Television program).
5. Television producers and directors–Canada–Biography. I. Brophy,
Mike, 1957- II. Title.
GV848.5.M45A3 2007   796.092   C2007-903070-X

CONTENTS

To all the Mellanbys — a legendary family.
— R.M.

To Marilyn — You are my inspiration and
the love of my life. Your support is unending
and always greatly appreciated.
— M.B.

FOREWORD

It seems like only yesterday that I got a call from Ralph Mellanby to be part of *Hockey Night in Canada*. I had just been fired by the Colorado Rockies and really had no job. I remember, on my first "Coach's Corner," I said, "I think the Leafs will make the playoffs." Ralph came in after the show, slammed his hand on the desk and said, "I *never* want to hear you say 'think' again! You're the coach and you should *know* — and if you're wrong, you're wrong."

I found out later that the CBC wanted to fire me a month into the season. They said they owed it to the English-speaking children of Canada. Ralph said, "If he goes, I go," and seeing that Ralph had just won an Emmy for the 1980 Olympics, which he produced, we both stayed. If it hadn't been for Ralph, my television career would have been over before it began.

Another time, a producer told me that he was upset about the way I pronounced players' names. Ralph just laughed and said, "Don't worry about it. That's half your charm." Ralph also produced the *Don Cherry's Grapevine* show, which ran for five years. I have to admit that he literally had to hold my hand, I was so nervous trying to do the opening of my show. I just couldn't get it. Finally, he said, "Just look at the picture of Blue and pretend you're talking to Blue." Bingo! I was off to the races.

Everything I have, I owe to Ralph. He laid his job on the line for me, guided me through the tough times. He's the best.

Ralph's only parting advice when he left *Hockey Night in Canada* was "Never turn professional" — and if you've seen me on television, you know I followed his advice.

Ralph has a million great stories to tell, and I know you're going to enjoy every one of them.

— *Don Cherry*

INTRODUCTION

The National Hockey League has produced more than its share of superstars, both on and off the ice.

Without question, the most famous have been players — Wayne Gretzky, Bobby Orr, Gordie Howe, Maurice Richard and many others. But in Canada, it's not only the players whose achievements have endeared them to the public. For decades, Foster Hewitt and Danny Gallivan brought hockey into Canadian living rooms with their colourful play-by-play. *Hockey Night in Canada* host Ron MacLean gets recognized everywhere he goes. And is there a bigger star in Canadian television than Don Cherry? Not a chance.

In hockey circles, the name of Ralph Mellanby is synonymous with quality and innovation in television. During a distinguished career that has taken him to all corners of the world, Mellanby has worked in the fields of news, sports and entertainment with every major North American network. He has covered thirteen Olympic Games, and his work has earned him five Emmy Awards. He was also named Canada's Broadcaster of the Year in 1990. But he is best known for his work as executive producer of *Hockey Night in Canada*, consistently one of the highest-rated television shows in the country. For more than two decades, the adventurous and innovative Mellanby brought Canada's favourite pastime into living rooms from coast to coast.

Ralph Mellanby is to television what the Orrs, Howes and Gretzkys are to hockey, and along the way he worked with some of the biggest names in the game — players, coaches, general managers and television personalities alike. *Walking with Legends* takes us behind the scenes, recounting his encounters with many of those who shaped the game, as well as his involvement in some of the greatest events in hockey's history, from the 1972 Summit Series to the 1980 Miracle on Ice at the Winter Olympics in Lake Placid.

* * *

Born in Hamilton, Ontario, in 1934, Mellanby lived there for eleven years before moving to Windsor and ultimately, two years later, to a farm in Essex. The son of a father who was a newspaperman and a mother who was a professional singer, Mellanby came from a family of gifted athletes and was a sports fanatic from the time he could walk. He was a good athlete, and played baseball, football and basketball. In fact, his school basketball team won the All-Ontario Championship in 1954 at Maple Leaf Gardens, beating Toronto's St. Michael's. Basketball was fun, but baseball was his best game; he played in a men's league beginning at age fifteen, and was ultimately scouted by the St. Louis Cardinals organization.

A career in professional baseball didn't pan out, but Mellanby grew fascinated with the idea of working in the media. His television career began when he took a part-time job as a prop boy at CKLW in Windsor while he attended college full time. He then decided that he would major in television — which didn't make his dad, a newspaper guy, especially happy.

The young Ralph, on the other hand, was delighted with each step he took during his career. "Every job I took, I thought it would be for the rest of my life," Mellanby says. "When I became a cameraman, I thought, 'I'll always be a cameraman' — I loved it. Then, when I became a technical director, I loved that and thought I'd always be a technical director. Then I became a director…"

Mellanby eventually moved across the river to Detroit to work with Soupy Sales on his local television show. Though he dabbled in sports, Mellanby was convinced his career path was directing him into the entertainment field. He had already directed a Petula Clark special.

"I wanted to be the next Norm Jewison," he says. "I'm still hoping to do a movie."

In 1966, however, he received a call that changed his life. The sponsors of *Hockey Night in Canada* were unhappy with the show, particularly the games originating out of Montreal, and felt the show needed to be jazzed up. They wanted somebody with a background in entertainment to take control of the show.

"There was only one thing that would keep me in Canada: hockey," Mellanby says. "I got a call from Ted Hough, the president of Canadian Sports Network, and he said, 'I don't think you'll be interested, but we're going to have our first executive producer on *Hockey Night in Canada*.' He asked me to meet with him in Montreal. When we sat down to talk about the job, I decided to request the most outlandish terms of a contract that I could make, just to see how serious they were.

"I really pushed the envelope, asking for free gas (I should have asked for free beer and a new car!), five trips a year for my wife, total moving allowance if I had to move (which I eventually did, from Montreal to Toronto). I got a call a week later and I was told they couldn't pay me any more than they would pay a senior advertising account executive, and I remember thinking that I'd blown it. It turns out, though, that the money I asked for wasn't much more than they were paying these guys.

"I told my wife, Janet, I had landed my dream job. I've done a million other things since, but *Hockey Night in Canada* was the biggest show in Canada at the time. Plus I had a vision of what the show needed."

Ralph Mellanby met stars, made stars and became a star.

Mellanby had worked in American television and decided that *Hockey Night in Canada* needed to be more about show business. However, he did encounter a little resistance from the old guard.

"I remember standing on a street in Toronto with an executive from *Hockey Night in Canada*, and I said, 'This is going to be a sensational year for *Hockey Night in Canada*,'" Mellanby recalls. "He turned to me and said, 'I think the last twenty years have been sensational.' That's the type of attitude I was up against. We needed more pizzazz in the show, and more than anything else we needed more editorial content. We had to become the image of the NHL and take on tough issues. Expansion was just around the corner and the game was going to grow. I knew we would never be able to sell the Minnesota North Stars or St. Louis Blues with glitz, because they had been mostly a bunch of minor-leaguers and were unknown."

Mellanby's timing was perfect. He arrived at *Hockey Night in Canada* right around the time that colour television was being introduced and the technology of the medium was taking off. The slow-motion replay had just been invented, and Mellanby made sure the show had the most up-to-date directional microphones and sound equipment — and don't forget about Howie Meeker's famous telestrator.

"Over the next few years, I forced the network to purchase the newest equipment because the sponsors — Imperial Oil, Molson and Ford — backed me," he says. "They told me we had to be the leader in the industry. That was the only mandate I ever got from their heads of marketing and advertising: *Hockey Night in Canada* had to be the best show and the leader of Canadian sports television."

Mellanby knew *Hockey Night in Canada* would never be a leader with the same tired old faces on camera, so he slowly began weeding out the weak links and replacing them with younger, more talented personnel.

Frank Selke Jr. left his position as the show's Montreal host to become president of the Oakland Seals (he would later return as a top executive at *Hockey Night*). Mellanby hired Dan Kelly and Dick Irvin, both young and talented, in Montreal. Irvin, the son of the legendary coach of the Montreal Canadiens, Toronto Maple Leafs and Chicago Black Hawks, replaced Danny Gallivan's colour man, Keith Dancy, while Kelly served as host and backup play-by-play commentator. Mellanby also made the youthful Brian McFarlane the permanent colour commentator in Toronto. Before long, the long-time Toronto host Ward Cornell was released, to be replaced by Dave Hodge. The makeover was complete.

"The show needed a new look," Mellanby says. "It needed its own logo, its own signature and its own music. Those were some of the areas I targeted my first year — a *Hockey Night in Canada* brand."

Mellanby had a new, larger set (made of bright fibreglass) designed, and instituted new camera angles. He dressed his talent in made-to-measure powder-blue jackets that instantly gave them a sense of pride and a feeling of being part of a team.

"We developed the *Hockey Night in Canada* way of doing things," he says. "People grew to understand what I wanted and what I was striving to achieve. I wouldn't even need to be around. If something was happening, somebody would say, 'That's not the way Ralph wants it,' or 'Ralph would never do it that way.' You know you have something good when that happens."

Longtime between-periods analyst Howie Meeker says that everybody respected Mellanby, even if they didn't necessarily like him.

"Ralph was *Hockey Night in Canada*," Meeker says. "He put the teams together. He had the finest talent in every department, from producers to camera people to on-air people to technical crews. He loved talent and he had the good sense to leave them alone. He would say to me, 'Howard, you can say anything you want, but don't hang us.' He kept no pressure on anybody. If he got pressure from above, it stayed with Ralph. It never got below him."

In his book *Hanging It Out on Camera 3*, Malcolm G. Kelly writes:

> *You know those dramatic openings that are a regular feature of* Hockey Night *and most other sports shows these days? The shots of the scalpers and chestnut salesmen outside the arena, the wide look at the skyline, the people coming in through the turnstiles while a sonorous voice imparts to the television audience expository wisdom about the battle to come?*

That's Ralph Mellanby.
How about the sound of bone-crunching hits along
the boards, or the puck dinging off the goalpost?
That's Ralph Mellanby.

There was a day when National Hockey League executives did their best to control television. That changed when Mellanby arrived on the scene. He got the powers that be to understand the importance of television in terms of promoting their game.

"For Ralph Mellanby not to be in the Hockey Hall of Fame is a disgrace," says Mark Askin, then a producer with *HNiC*, in *Hanging It Out on Camera 3*. "He had more to do with the growth of hockey than almost any of the other builders."

Although Mellanby has done much more in television than just hockey, *Walking with Legends* concentrates on one aspect of his long and decorated career: his time with *Hockey Night in Canada*.

— *Mike Brophy*

PART I
ON THE AIR

Chapter 1

THE PIONEERS FOSTER AND BILL HEWITT

Foster Hewitt was already a legend by the time I met him in the early 1960s. Heck, he was a legend when I was a little boy. The pioneer of hockey broadcasting — with his high-pitched catch phrase "He shoots! He scores!" — was very familiar to millions of hockey fans across Canada and the United States. When you listened to Foster calling the play-by-play on radio, you saw the action through his eyes.

In the 1930s and '40s, everybody listened to Foster Hewitt. He was the biggest thing in hockey. Everybody wanted to be Foster Hewitt. In those days, there was no television — there was only radio. Few people ever actually saw Charlie Conacher play, but thanks to Foster, countless fans could imagine they had. He was the link between the players and the fans, and you learned whatever you knew about the players from him. Foster used to say, "There was never a bad game when I broadcast it." That was his attitude, and it served him well in a career that began in 1923 and concluded in 1978.

It is not an overstatement to say that Foster Hewitt was one of the most famous men in Canada. You need to remember that, when Foster began calling the action on radio, most people didn't leave their homes on Saturday nights. It's not like today, when people have so many options as to how they'll spend their time and money. In Foster's heyday, people didn't have a lot of money to spare, and radio was a primary source of entertainment. Foster grabbed his listeners with his famous opening — "Hello, Canada, and hockey fans in the United States and Newfoundland" — and didn't relinquish his grip until the game was over. During the war years, recordings of his broadcasts were sent abroad to improve troop morale.

Were if not for him, I wouldn't have had my job as executive producer of *Hockey Night in Canada*. I've never lost sight of that fact. He created the template for hockey broadcasting. Similarly, the older announcers, like Bob Cole and Danny Gallivan, grew up listening to Foster and, of course, they emulated him. Foster knew how to raise or lower his voice with the rhythm of the game, and in the process he all but invented play-by-play.

Using a telephone, Foster called his first hockey game on February 16, 1923, a contest between the Toronto Argonauts and Kitchener Greenshirts at the Mutual Street Arena. When the Toronto Maple Leafs were formed in 1927, Foster became their announcer. And he called the action of the very first televised NHL game, between the Maple Leafs and Boston Bruins, on November 1, 1952.

When I got the job with *HNiC*, Foster was still doing play-by-play on radio, but he would join our television broadcast at the conclusion of each game to name the three stars. He was the one who initiated the tradition of choosing three stars from each game, and the tradition carries on to this day. Eventually, Foster crossed over and started calling the action on television. He would work with his son Bill, who followed in his dad's footsteps and became another excellent announcer. They would switch back and forth between television and radio, with Foster calling the action on television in the first period while Bill did radio. Then they'd switch jobs. It was kind of an unusual way to operate, but it worked.

I didn't really have a lot to do with Foster when I was directing games on *Hockey Night*. In fact, I had a hard time getting to know our two big announcers — Hewitt and Gallivan, the legends — because they never attended meetings. Foster and Danny would just do their thing, somewhat anonymously. You wouldn't see them before, during or even after the games. I found that quite frustrating. It was a strange way of working with people, and it was something I worked to change. Sports television was not very sophisticated back then, which was one of the main reasons I was hired to run *Hockey Night in Canada*: to bring the kind of production values that were seen in entertainment programming, as well as to pick up the pace and inject some journalism into the show.

I decided very early on that, regardless of his status, I was in charge now and Foster was going to have to do things a new way. Prior to this time, nobody had ever really spoken with Foster about how he worked. I arranged to meet with him at the Westbury Hotel in Toronto, around the corner from Maple Leaf Gardens, and I'm not certain if I was expecting a battle, but I must say I came away with a very good impression of him. In fact, I found him to be quiet and very humble ... almost a little insecure.

"What I want to do with you, Foster," I began, "is to bring a makeup girl upstairs, so when you come off radio, in the minute and a half between the end of the game and you doing the three stars, I'll have her make you look good for television. I want you to look like a million bucks when you come on to do the stars." It was 1966 — colour television had been introduced by then, and I wanted Foster to look colourful. (That was also when we introduced the blue blazers with the *Hockey Night in Canada* logo embroidered on them.)

Foster looked at me and said, "Ralph, you are the first guy who has ever talked to me about television. I want to be better."

I was relieved to hear that, if not a little shocked — he had been on television since 1952!

I appreciated the trust Foster had in me and the fact that he took direction. He was a legend, but not a prima donna.

I told Foster, "You're famous for always picking the goalie of the winning team as the first star, the goalie of the other team if it's a close game ... I don't want that. This is your segment. You are Foster Hewitt. You *are* hockey! Let's make this better."

We worked on it, and it helped the show and it helped Foster.

It also marked the beginning of a great relationship between Foster and myself.

Foster loved the blue *HNiC* blazer. When we went on the road, he would always wear that jacket, even to dinner. *Hockey Night in Canada* was his claim to fame — indeed, it was Foster who coined the title of the show — and he quite enjoyed the notoriety.

In 1972, he came out of retirement to call the action of the fabled Summit Series between the NHL's top stars and the best players from the Soviet Union. Because he'd been away for so long, Foster was really worried about pronouncing the Russian names properly. Once again he came to me.

I got Aggie Kukulowicz, who spoke Russian and served as an interpreter during the series, to record all the Russian names on tape with the proper pronunciation, and Foster memorized them. It was a mixed crew, one half from CTV and the other half from CBC. Johnny Esaw and Pat Marsden served as the game hosts, while Brian Conacher provided colour commentary alongside Foster.

I didn't give the tape to Conacher, because he was a CTV guy (though Brian was smart enough to get the proper pronunciations for himself when he worked with me at the 1976 Olympics). Foster was my guy, from *Hockey Night in Canada*. He took the tape to the radio station he started, CKFH, and listened to it over and over again.

I also gave the tape to Howie Meeker, our analyst for the series, but he still didn't get the Russian names right.

I think Foster did a great job in that series. It should have come as no surprise that he rose to the occasion. The classic Foster Hewitt sound, with the ups and downs, the highs and lows that I loved to hear, was fully in evidence. It's what set him apart from most who call play-by-play action.

The funny thing is, Foster nailed the Russian pronunciations perfectly, but struggled with some of the NHL stars' names! He could say Kharlamov (pronounced har-la-mov), but stumbled when it came time to say Cournoyer. He would pronounce it "crun-ooy-eh."

The fans didn't care — they loved him and were delighted to

have the opportunity to hear the old master once again.

It was tough for him to travel across Canada and to the Soviet Union, but he pulled it off like the true professional he was.

* * *

When it came time to celebrate the fiftieth anniversary of Maple Leaf Gardens in 1981, I decided I wanted Foster to be on the ice as part of the pre-game ceremony. He had been on the ice the night the building opened, and I felt it was fitting that he be part of this occasion. Here's the funny thing: he told me he hadn't been on the ice at the Gardens since opening night. That blew me away.

I went to Leafs owner Harold Ballard, but he wasn't keen on the idea.

"That shifty son of a bitch!" Ballard said. "There's no way he's getting out on the ice. He's the last who'll get on the ice. That guy has made more money than Stafford, Connie and myself combined... He still has his first nickel. He's the richest son of a bitch around."

I don't really know why Harold didn't like Foster. Maybe he figured Foster made too much money broadcasting the Leafs' games over CKFH.

I worked on Ballard, and he finally relented. I told him Foster's appearance would make for great television, and we'd have shots of Harold sitting in his bunker (located in the wall at the south end of the building). "We'll play you up," I said, "give you lots of air time on TV." That helped.

When the night finally arrived, Foster was excited. If you watch a tape of the ceremonies, you will see Foster standing at the side of the ice, by the boards, and I'm holding his hand. He was, of course, wearing his blue *Hockey Night* jacket.

When Gardens announcer Paul Morris said, "Ladies and gentlemen, please welcome Foster Hewitt," the Gardens absolutely erupted.

The Maple Leafs didn't have many heroes — not like the Montreal Canadiens. When the Canadiens did something, they could parade out their legends — Jean Beliveau, Rocket Richard, Dickie Moore, Boom Boom Geoffrion, Elmer Lach, Butch Bouchard ... you could go on and on. That was not the case in Toronto. The organization didn't really have the mystique that you might have thought it did.

Foster was a major exception to the rule. He stepped out onto the ice and the noise was deafening. I stood there and cried. The love the people in the crowd felt for this pioneer, this dedicated professional, was undeniable. I wonder if Harold, as crusty as he was on the outside, had an appreciation for what was unfolding in his home before him?

Foster stepped off the ice, looking great, and turned and winked at me as if to say, "Thanks. That was great."

* * *

Foster worked around the corner from the Gardens at his radio station, CKFH. As Harold alluded to, he had a reputation as the cheapest guy in the world, but I will say that he always bought lunch when I was with him. I would offer to pay, because I was on an expense account, but he would say, "No. I asked you to lunch, and I'll pay."

He became like a second father to me. He was always there to lend a hand if I asked him. He attended a fundraiser for minor hockey in my hometown of Essex, Ontario, and later called the action for the very first old-timers' game between the Canadiens and Maple Leafs. That particular game was to be televised, and I thought, even though he was retired, it would be fantastic if we could get him to call the play-by-play. He said, "I'll do it, but I want to take the train down the night before, like I used to, and you are coming with me."

That was Foster, reliving the good old days.

* * *

I decided I wanted to produce a record album of all of the highlights from *Hockey Night in Canada*, but many of the old recordings — featuring some of the greatest moments in hockey history — were lost. It always bothered me that we didn't have much of an archive from the old days. "Well," Foster said, "I'll just recreate them."

"How can you remember all those plays?" I wondered.

"I just close my eyes and I see it all."

I wanted to recreate the first game ever, from the Mutual Street Arena, and we wanted it to sound authentic. So, instead of recording the play-by-play in the studio, he walked downstairs to a phone booth on the corner.

"This is the opening game from Mutual Street Arena..." he said into the phone, and we recorded it.

We did find some stuff he had saved over the years, but I would say that 80 percent of the record was recreated. Danny Gallivan did his share for the record, and so did Bill Hewitt, but nobody was as good as Foster.

* * *

It may be surprising to learn that Foster had a great sense of humour. He loved to joke about money and his reputation for being cheap. After the fundraiser in Essex, a bunch of us — Dave Hodge, Brian McFarlane, Howie Meeker and, of course, Foster — went to see the school I had attended.

A girl who used to be, uh, quite popular with the boys, if you know what I mean, took us on a tour of the school. She was showing Foster all the old pictures and was really chatting him up. As we were leaving, Foster said, "That was great, Ralph. I really enjoyed that."

When we were all sitting in the limo on the way back to the hotel, he added, "That girl was so lovely ... taking me around the school and showing me all the photos and trophies."

"Well, Foster," I said, "you know that at one time she was kind to everybody — if you know what I mean."

Without skipping a beat, Foster said, "Well, why are we leaving?"

Although he is best known for broadcasting hockey games, Foster also occasionally called the action for Canadian Football League games and other sporting events. Once, while calling the Grey Cup game in Toronto, Foster — wearing a big fur coat — announced from the roof of Varsity Stadium. He actually froze to his spot. The only way he could leave was by ruining the coat, ripping it from the roof.

As a play-by-play man, Foster was disciplined. Once he did something he felt was right, that's the way he would do it for all time. His broadcasts were a point of personal pride, and it bothered him that announcers at local stations across the country — especially out west — would steal his broadcasts. They would listen to his call of the game and then simply repeat what he said. One night, in the middle of a broadcast, Foster announced a goal that hadn't actually been scored. The copycats were caught red-handed when they repeated the report of the goal. Then Foster came back and said that the goal had been waved off.

I was always working to promote and market *Hockey Night in Canada*, so I was allowed to bring people into the studio. It could be anyone from movie stars to politicians to entertainers to presidents of major companies. Stars came to the Gardens and always wanted to take a tour — especially to see "the gondola."

I told Foster, "People want to meet you, and I'd like you to be the end of my tour. It will be at the end of the second period ... you'll be finishing radio and I'll bring them in to meet you." I'd also take these guests into the truck where the game was being produced and directed. The guys in the truck hated it, but the guests always found it fascinating. And when they met Foster, all of them — men and women alike — were speechless. I would look at them and could just tell they were thinking, "I just met God!" Foster always made them feel welcome, and he would go to the trouble of finding out who was coming so that he could say something special. For instance, it might be Anne Murray visiting the gondola, and he'd say, "I love your music. You're my favourite singer." Although he didn't seem to have a favourite politician...

* * *

When Bobby Orr and I filmed the "Hockey Legends" series in Jamaica, Orr said, "The one guy I *really* want is Foster Hewitt." I said to Bobby, "We've got to get more than we need on Foster."

Bobby asked why.

"There's not enough archival stuff on Foster," I replied. "We have to get all the great stories we can from him."

In the end, we wound up doing Foster as a two-parter, broadcasting the segments on back-to-back weeks on *HNiC*.

When it came time to do the interview, in July, it was extremely hot. Bobby treated Foster like gold. It was so hot, Bobby said, "Where's an umbrella for Foster? We can't have him out in the heat like this."

I said, "We don't have anybody to carry the umbrella."

"I'll carry it," Bobby insisted.

And he did carry it while we filmed scenes of the two walking together. Bobby would pamper Foster. He made us take breaks whenever he felt that Foster was getting tired.

Foster was there for a full week, and he liked to have a drink or two. I went to him the night before we began filming his segment and said, "Foster, you can't be drinking the day before, the night before or the day we shoot."

"Ralph, I hear you," he said. "Don't worry."

During the filming, he was great — the old pro! And I know he never touched a drop. He was perfect. He was professional. But the night immediately after we finished, I think he made up for lost time...

Imagine: I had the privilege of doing two shows with hockey's greatest player and the world's greatest broadcaster!

When Foster died, CBC Radio asked me to describe, in thirty seconds, what Foster Hewitt meant to hockey.

I said, "I don't need thirty seconds. Foster Hewitt was *Hockey Night in Canada* and every hockey broadcaster alive owes a debt to him."

I don't think he ever really understood how much he meant to others.

* * *

Foster's son Bill also called play-by-play, for thirty years. I tried to give Bill everything he wanted (for instance, he loved the Playboy Clubs, and in every city we'd travel to he would always drag me along). In return, he gave me what I wanted.

Foster invented the form and had a passion for it, but for Bill it was more of a job. That's not to suggest he didn't love and care about what he did. It just wasn't the same — and why would it be? Did hockey mean the same to Mark or Marty Howe as it did to their dad, Gordie? Of course not.

Bill was different. He never really fit in with the guys on the crew. I always thought Bill was a kind soul — he wasn't Foster, he wasn't show business, he was just Bill who really wanted to be a farmer, not a celebrity.

I treated him with the utmost respect, but the other guys used to laugh at him behind his back. That always bothered me. I tried to build him up. Anytime I ever said anything about him in the media, I made sure I was kind. He wasn't Foster, but you know what? In terms of calling games, there was nobody better. He never made a mistake on the air, right up until the very end. When he got up inside the gondola, he did his job very efficiently. The thing is, neither he nor Foster ever got very close to the players.

He *would* say funny things — though not intentionally, of course. Once, when he was checking into a hotel with his fiancée — keeping in mind that people were sensitive to unmarried couples cohabiting in those days — he registered as Mr. and Mrs. Bill Hewitt. Just as he was signing the register, the rest of the crew wandered into the hotel and Bill shouted, "Hey guys, have you met my fiancée?"

Bill wasn't one for appearing on camera. It had to be a special occasion before he'd go on. Bill would have been lost today, because most play-by-play announcers enjoy a lot of camera time, especially between periods.

On one occasion, Audrey Phillips, who was a longtime script assistant and a wonderful person whom Bill absolutely loved, was going to be at a game, seated in the stands. Audrey had been in the hospital for an operation and had been off the show for half a season.

During production meetings, Bill never had much to offer. He would attend them, but he would sit there idly until the meeting ended, then go and do his job. On this occasion, I told Bill that I had invited Audrey to be our guest at the game, and we were going to take a shot of her on television.

"Ah, that's wonderful," Bill said.

At the end of the meeting, I said, "Does anybody have anything to add?"

Bill piped up: "Yes. When they take the shot of Audrey, I would like to say something [on camera]."

Now, Bill never did anything like this. Brian McFarlane always handled these chores.

"Okay," I said. And all the guys in the meeting rolled their eyes as if to say, "uh-oh."

That night, I was in the truck, producing the show, and I wanted to get Audrey on early. I didn't leave anything to chance: I'd written something out for Bill to say on the air. At the appropriate moment, I said into Bill's ear, "Bill, we're coming out of commercial and we're going to take the shot of Audrey Phillips. Are you ready to talk?"

"Yes."

So we put the camera on Audrey, and … nothing. Bill didn't say a word. He froze. He must have lost the script I'd prepared for him.

Here we had a shot of this woman and her husband sitting in the stands, with no explanation as to why we were showing them. The viewers must have wondered what the heck was up.

In the next period, I told Bill we were going to try again. We took another shot of Audrey and, again, nothing. Bill froze again.

At this point, I was getting a little antsy about the situation, so I told Bill, "We're going to have to do that again. She may not be staying for the whole game."

By now, Audrey was getting more airtime than Darryl Sittler. The audience must have wondered if she was the producer's mistress or something, since every time we showed her there was no explanation of who she was.

I figured we'd try one more time in the second period. So we put the camera on her one more time and I said, "Bill, there's Audrey in the crowd."

Into his microphone, Bill said, "There's Audrey in the crowd."

The whole crew in the truck was rolling on the ground in laughter. The audience, however, could only be confused.

Before the period ended, I said to McFarlane, "You do it." I also said, "Bill, shut up."

Brian, the ultimate pro, told the audience who Audrey was and how much she meant to *Hockey Night in Canada*.

That's why you never gave Bill anything special to accomplish.

His final night was an absolute disaster. He had a nervous breakdown on the air. He pretty much had every player who ever played for the Leafs playing that night.

It was one of the saddest nights of my life. There was a lot of speculation about Bill — that he was drunk or on drugs. I don't believe that was the case.

That night, Bill left the Gardens and never came back.

Brian McFarlane took over after the first period and proved why he was so valuable. He could do anything, even play-by-play.

I thought Bill might return to the broadcast booth, but he never did. Instead, he lived a very pleasant life on his farm. I would visit him and we would talk about old times. He loved it! He died a very happy man.

What happened on that last night in the gondola does not diminish what he accomplished throughout a long, productive career. He was a great announcer. That's why he and Foster are the only father-and-son combination to be honoured by the Hockey Hall of Fame's broadcast wing.

It always bugged me that the guys who worked with Bill Hewitt treated him poorly. That wasn't right. It was sad. Here was a guy who just wanted to be part of the team, but the other players on that team wouldn't have it. I was heartbroken. Worst of all, Hewitt's departure came and went, and it was as if nobody cared. We weren't inundated with letters. Nobody asked about him. I never understood why. He had been on the broadcasts for so many years, and now it was as if he was a nonentity. He was like General McArthur — he just faded away.

Chapter 2

THE CONSUMMATE PRO BRIAN MCFARLANE

> "The best sports production in the world is *Hockey Night in Canada*, and their best is Brian McFarlane. That's why we got him." — Scotty Connal, executive producer of NBC Sports, on hiring Brian McFarlane for NBC hockey telecasts

The first time I met Brian McFarlane was in 1959 when we were both working the CBS *Game of the Week*. I was freelancing as a cameraman, and he was doing the intermission — on skates — at the old Detroit Olympia with Bud Palmer. We talked a few minutes during the taping, and little did either of us know it would be the beginning of a long, rewarding relationship.

A few years later, in 1961, we both ended up in Montreal. Brian was the sports director at CFCF television, and I was a director, mainly on CTV's football coverage, but also making some ventures into entertainment, directing variety shows. It was a new station, and we operated out of a temporary studio while our new studios were being built. Being the new kid in town, I wanted to get to know all the guys who were going to be working on the network — especially Brian. Getting a network off the ground is a lot of work, but we had fun. In fact, we put together a bowling team, the Channel 12 Chickens, in an effort to get ourselves known in the community. We also played on the station's softball team together.

I learned quickly what a bright, intelligent guy he was — far more than an everyday jock. We'd often go over to the tavern for lunch, across the road from our temporary studio. He was an Ottawa Valley boy and, of course, I was from southern Ontario. He would tell me about his dad, Leslie McFarlane, who wrote twenty-one Hardy Boys books under the pseudonym Franklin W. Dixon, as well as a number of others under names such as Carolyn Keene and Roy Rockwood. All were huge sellers, so Brian evidently had the writing gene in his blood.

We palled around, always talking about what we'd like to do in the future. I also soon realized that we had something in common: we both hated the corporate world and really longed for a freelance existence with lots of freedom. I also appreciated Brian's love for sports.

After we finally got the station on the air, Dick Irvin — whom I didn't know very well at the time — would pop in every now and then to guest on Brian's sports shows. One day, Brian came up to me in the CFCF cafeteria and said, "I'm going to hire Dick to do local sports with me. I've got a lot of choices, but I think I'll take Dick and teach him the business."

Brian finally grew frustrated at being promised pay raises and not receiving them and being promised extra money for doing additional assignments and not getting it, so he left the station to work at CFTO in Toronto. When that happened, Dick Irvin became our sports director. I felt bad for Brian because he was one of the early stars at the station. Eventually he joined *Hockey Night in Canada*, which was my good fortune because Brian, who was doing colour commentary, and Morley Kells, who was the creative surge on *Hockey Night*, pushed for me to get the position of director. Morley had told a friend, "If we get Ralph in here to be the head honcho in production, he'll understand our ideas. He'll understand what we want to do if we want to change the show."

Because I had directed for *Hockey Night* on CTV, it wasn't as if I was totally unknown to the brass. I was mainly doing variety shows at the time, but that meant I was considered a good fit for the new position because they were looking for a production mindset that was new, forward-thinking and had a touch of showbiz. As I later learned, Jack Burkholder, who was a big shot at Imperial Oil, said, "There is only one choice here — a director who does news and sports but also works with dancers and singers like Petula Clark, Frankie Laine and Nat King Cole. That's what *Hockey Night* needs, so get him!"

Brian and Morley were happy when I got the job. They felt I was one of them. But I think they might have been disappointed when they found out that I didn't want to radically change the show immediately. Frankly, I didn't want to break the mould. "I don't want to knock down the walls," I told Brian. "I just want to put a crack in them, or else we'll fail." That said, I was fortunate to have Brian there, because he told me all kinds of things about working on *Hockey Night* that made my life easier.

Morley was eventually dropped because many of his ideas were too radical — too "far out" for the sponsors. Brian, however, grew into a star. He had the same vision for the show as I did. We didn't want to be run-of-the-mill. We wanted more editorial content and to be creative, and Brian, because he was educated and had vision, was the right partner for us to achieve our mutual ambitions.

Brian could do play-by-play, colour commentary and work on the panel between periods on both radio and television. He also worked with Foster Hewitt at the end of games. He could write, and he had great ideas for the show. I often used Brian for voice-overs, writing or to host "Showdown in the NHL." Anytime we did a special, Brian was my first choice to be part of the show, and he always had a feel for what it should be like. That applied to "Pro Tips," "Showdown" or "Countdown to Face-Off." I also feel he could have been a great producer, had he elected to try his hand at that. People used to jokingly call him "Brian McMapleLeaf," which I used to laugh about, because they associated him with Leafs broadcasts. But I didn't think that was a fair assessment. He wasn't a Leaf guy, he was a *Hockey Night in Canada* guy. Brian was an unbiased pro who later went on to be the host of Montreal Canadiens games and also found his way to Winnipeg, Calgary and Edmonton broadcasts.

He was — and is — a great public speaker, so he became a great representative of *HNiC* at functions. Whenever we got a request for a speaker, we would always get Brian to do it and throw a few bucks his way. I'd tell Brian what I expected and he'd follow directions. He appeared all over the country on behalf of *Hockey Night*. He also brought the Bank of Nova Scotia — with whom he'd worked on the Scotiabank Hockey College — on board as a big sponsor for the program.

Brian worked well with Bill Hewitt. They were a real team — Bill was greatly improved by having Brian at his side. Brian's comments always added to Bill's commentary and made him look good. Their work stands up today. Because of his versatility, I could move him onto any crew and he would always be a good fit.

I used to enjoy it when we would get to broadcast a "neutral" series (one that didn't involve a Canadian team), because I could put together my dream team in the broadcast booth. The first time that happened was in 1968, when the St. Louis Blues played the Minnesota North Stars in the West Division finals.

St. Louis coach Scotty Bowman came up to me at one point and said, "Well, I guess we're not good enough for the number one crew — there's no Danny Gallivan."

I said, "Scotty, this is history. We're using our young guys, just like you — Irvin, Kelly and McFarlane." Today, all three have been honoured by the Hockey Hall of Fame.

* * *

Brian's biggest strength, however, was also his downfall. He would take up causes, and in doing so, he brought a lot to the show that I liked. But occasionally he'd go too far and I'd have to reel him in. I think I had a better feel for how far we could go on the show. Brian was always hell-bent and would go to the wall.

Once, during a Leafs broadcast, Toronto's Forbes Kennedy did something on the ice and Brian piped up, "He's going to be suspended for doing that!"

Well, NHL president Clarence Campbell was furious. How dare a *Hockey Night in Canada* broadcaster tell him how to do his job? But Brian wasn't telling Campbell how to do his job; he was just expressing his opinion. Mr. Campbell called and said, "Who the hell is he to say what I should or should not do?"

I must say, my boss, Ted Hough, showed a lot of courage. He told Campbell, "I think he should be complimented for saying what he thought. That's our new way."

And the next day, Kennedy was suspended by the league.

Nowadays, nobody thinks twice about broadcasters voicing their opinion, but back then it wasn't done. The owners and the league didn't get it. They didn't understand that broadcasters had to say what they thought. That's what I wanted from my talent.

Brian continued to be something of a rebel, always speaking his mind. He'd say something derogatory about the Maple Leafs, and the team's feisty owner, Harold Ballard, would call me.

"I want Brian off the show!" Ballard would scream. I'd have to fight him on it, and I usually won. There were times, though, when we'd have to pretend to suspend him for doing or saying something the owners didn't like.

In a way, it's strange how Ballard was always on Brian's case. The funny thing is, Harold always wanted to be controversial, but he hated it when other people took up that mantle.

Once, on our season-opening broadcast in Winnipeg, we asked to interview Leafs captain Darryl Sittler between periods. That summer, Ballard had tried to prevent his players from appearing in our "Showdown" show, which we had taped in the summer for broadcast during the season. The end result of that dispute was that Sittler stepped down as Leafs captain.

Leafs general manager Punch Imlach came into the truck while I was producing, and I had to ask him to step outside because I didn't want the guys in the truck to hear the argument. Imlach told me we couldn't have Sittler — not with McFarlane as the host.

"If it was anybody else but McFarlane doing the interview, I'd let you have him," Imlach said. He figured that with anybody else the interview would be more mundane, but that Brian would somehow bring out Sittler's anger about his ongoing fued with Imlach.

We ended up getting Laurie Boschman, who was from Saskatchewan, as our guest. I talked to Brian on his headset during a commercial break and told him I had changed guests, from Sittler to Boschman. I said I'd explain later why we had to make the switch. Later, Brian and I had it out. He wanted Sittler on the show and was furious that we'd caved in to Imlach and the Leafs. Brian was right, but given the politics of the matter, I had still made the wise move.

When we got back to Toronto, all hell broke loose because Brian said something to a newspaper reporter defending Sittler. (Imagine what would've happened if Sittler *had* appeared with Brian on the broadcast from Winnipeg!) I got a call from Ted Hough, and was told that Brian was off the show. Dick Beddoes, the legendary sportswriter and Harold's good friend, intervened to help get Brian back on *HNiC*. He went to Harold and pleaded Brian's case, saying that he was putting his kids through college, etc. Harold relented somewhat, saying that Brian could appear on the show, but that he couldn't be the colour man.

I had set my crew for the broadcast, thinking that Brian wasn't going to be part of it, but I later decided to write him into it. We put him outside Maple Leaf Gardens and pre-taped the opening to make sure everything was right.

Two guys walked by as Brian was taping, and one said, "Hey, there's Brian McFarlane. Harold won't let him into the Gardens. He has to do all his work outside."

"Jesus," the other guy said, "come January he's going to be cold as hell."

When NBC began broadcasting hockey, I told them Brian should be their number one choice as host. He had gone to St. Lawrence

University, where he was an All-America hockey star, and he'd worked on U.S. network broadcasts before. So where Brian originally helped me get on *Hockey Night,* I had a hand in getting him back on the air in the States via Scotty Connal, their executive producer. It also helped that I was to direct their show and help them get started at NBC.

Brian wanted to teach kids about hockey, so he came up with Peter Puck, a cartoon character who instantly became hugely popular upon his debut in 1974 on *Hockey Night* and NBC's *Game of the Week.* Brian created and wrote the series, while I produced it in association with the people from Hanna-Barbera in Hollywood — the animator who worked on Peter Puck used to do *The Flintstones.* It was fun and exciting to work in a new form. They didn't know a thing about hockey, so Brian and I guided them through it.

What I liked most about Brian was that he had a great sense of the history of the game. He is one of our most prolific writers of hockey books. Over the years, the only concern I had was that I had to be politically careful with Brian. It was worth the risk. Today, Brian is recognized on both sides of the border as one of history's great hockey broadcasters. I feel Brian could do any job to perfection, and I am proud to have worked alongside him and to have made *Hockey Night in Canada* the best sports production in the world.

Chapter 3

THE DREAM TEAM
DANNY GALLIVAN AND DICK IRVIN

> "I have never been around one broadcaster who doesn't swear, never mind two!" — Ron Harrison, director for *Hockey Night in Canada*

When I grew up in Essex, Ontario, our town was divided — you were either a fan of the Montreal Canadiens or you beat it. Because we were situated near Detroit, people assumed everybody in town cheered for the Red Wings, but that wasn't the case. Our town cheered for the Canadiens.

And nobody cheered for the Toronto Maple Leafs — don't ask me why!

So, as a kid I was for the Canadiens. (My brother, Jim, went against the grain a bit — he was a Red Wings fan.) To me, the Habs' play-by-play man, Danny Gallivan, was an iconic figure, and I loved listening to him call the action of my favourite team and favourite players. Unfortunately, most of the Saturday-night games we received were from Toronto, not Montreal. Because I had no real love for the Maple Leafs, the Hewitts didn't do much for me back then.

By the time I joined *Hockey Night in Canada*, Danny Gallivan was already a legend. I remember him as an elegant man, always impeccably dressed. A former teacher of English, he loved the language.

Originally, I directed him when *Hockey Night in Canada* was shown on CTV on Wednesday nights. I loved directing, but right from the start I couldn't figure Gallivan out. He wasn't a prima donna, but he could be awfully stubborn. He was an independent thinker, and a trifle eccentric. Suffice it to say our working relationship was not always a smooth one, and I blame myself for that. I never appreciated Danny as much as I should have. I looked at him as a radio guy who, like Foster Hewitt, never fully adapted to television.

To me, Danny wasn't flexible. Right from the start, we weren't on the same page. I liked him, but I hardly ever saw him because he wouldn't attend production meetings or the morning skates where reporters gathered information about the upcoming game. He had his regimen and he wasn't really interested in what others thought — especially not a young hotshot from Essex. It was frustrating, and I used to tell my bosses, "This is ridiculous." But they would simply say, "Foster Hewitt doesn't go to meetings, either. That's their routine, it's how they work. Get used to it." So I'd tell the late Keith Dancy — Danny's colour man — what we were going to do, and he'd say, "Don't worry. I'll tell Danny."

I would be left shaking my head.

When I became executive producer, my priority became putting together a solid team in Montreal — Toronto already had Bill Hewitt and Brian McFarlane in the booth, and the iconic Ward Cornell as host. My thinking was that I was the boss now and Danny was going to do things my way. How wrong I was! I tried to modernize him and make him into a television broadcaster. I made him come to production meetings. But I realized right away that we were oil and water. We argued constantly.

You have to remember that, when I started, I was also executive producer for radio. Danny was fine on radio, but television is more demanding. On radio — and it's just as true today as it was then — you just call the game. You could call the game in your pyjamas and no one would know. As Foster Hewitt once told me, "I never had a bad game on radio. I could make stuff up and no one would know. I could miss a player — who would know?" I didn't feel that Danny understood that he needed to approach television differently from radio.

I soon found out what others who had worked with Danny Gallivan already knew: he was his own man who had his own way, and he resisted my attempts to modernize him.

For example, when Danny started on television, he used an old hand-held microphone. When I took over as executive producer, I wanted Danny to wear one of the new headset mics so we could talk to him from the truck. He wanted no part of it. One of the other advantages of the new mics was that they gave us better sound. Danny had one pet peeve that he brought up every year: he said the organ in the Montreal Forum was too loud and it drowned him out.

"Well," I would tell him, "if you'd use the right mic, that wouldn't happen."

When I finally got him to wear the headset, there was a condition attached: he had to be allowed to keep holding his old mic. It was like his security blanket. We indulged him, but the mic wasn't plugged in.

Danny got into the booth for his first broadcast using the new equipment, and things were going smoothly until he said, "Ron Andrews [our statistician] is with us, and he's celebrating his twentieth year with *Hockey Night in Canada*."

Then he took the old mic — which wasn't plugged in — and handed it to Ron.

"Say a few words, Ron."

Of course, no one heard a single word Ron said.

The game continued with Danny calling the action — then suddenly, without warning, he coughed. Well, the new mic had a "cough switch" that cut off the mic when activated, but through force of habit, Danny covered the *old* mic. Naturally, his cough came through loud (very loud) and clear, and probably startled the audience.

After about five different things like this happened, I finally went up into the booth. Danny said, "I'm sorry. This won't happen again."

I said, "You're goddamn right it won't. I'm plugging in the

[hand-held] mic. That way, I have a backup."

He got used to the new equipment — as I knew he would — but he always had to have that old microphone with him. When he went on the road, so did his old mic.

When he retired, we had a party for him, and I had the microphone gold-plated and presented it to him. He was thrilled.

Looking back now, I realize I was way off base. I tried to change Danny, and it couldn't be done. Still, times were changing. Television was becoming more technical: slow-motion replay was being introduced, and games were now being broadcast in colour. Danny would always go off on his own. That's why I knew that I had to get him a great colour man who was also a great television broadcaster, someone Danny would come to love and respect. That was Dick Irvin.

When Irvin and Gallivan became a team, it meant I no longer had to worry about a lot of things. Dick would look after Danny and do the things I wanted to get done. They worked wonderfully together.

There were some curves, however. Danny would say things like, "That's three goals in forty-two seconds for the Canadiens. Dick, is that a new record?'

You could almost hear Dick flipping through the pages of the record book, but he always came up with the answer.

Danny and I did become great friends, however. The thing is, it had nothing to do with hockey or, for that matter, *Hockey Night in Canada*. Our friendship was based on our mutual love of golf and baseball. When we went on the road, particularly during the playoffs, we'd always go to a ballgame together — to Tiger Stadium in Detroit, or Fenway Park in Boston. When we got on the plane, all we'd talk about was baseball. We talked little about hockey.

Danny was very stubborn; probably one of the most stubborn guys I ever worked with. Every summer, I would meet with the broadcasters, and with Danny it was usually on the golf course. Year after year, he would raise two complaints, and he was right about one of them.

The first thing, as I've mentioned, was that he thought the Forum organ was too loud. The other was that he wasn't being paid enough. To win his confidence, I talked to my bosses, Frank Selke Jr. and Ted Hough, and convinced them to give Danny some security. So he got a five-year deal — no small matter, because everyone else besides Foster Hewitt was on a series of one-year contracts.

In the middle of it, he came to me and said he still wasn't making enough. He had encountered some marital problems, so his financial picture had changed. Still, I told him, "You agreed to the deal and you're making the most money of anybody on the show."

"But *they're* all underpaid!" he replied.

He would even make references to his money problems on the air. He'd say things like, "Well, Dick, I tried to cash my cheque the other day, and it was no problem at all because it wasn't much money."

Danny loved the English language, and he was an even better storyteller than he was a play-by-play man. One thing that drove me nuts, though, was the way he'd make words up. The public loved these Gallivanisms — like "cannonading" or "spinarama" — but not me.

At one meeting, I challenged him. "I've looked in every dictionary, and there's no such word as 'cannonading.'"

"There is now," was his response.

And, sure enough, if you look under "S" in the *Canadian Oxford Dictionary*, you'll find an entry for "spinarama."

* * *

A play-by-play man can only carry a broadcast so far. Even the best of them need solid sidemen — a colour analyst. Danny was no exception.

I first got to know Dick when he was a guest on a show I directed on CFCF in Montreal called *Sportsmen's Club*. Brian McFarlane was the host. Dick was a graduate of McGill and was working in accounting at the time, but he wanted to get into television. Brian, who was the sports director at CFCF, thought Dick had the potential to be a broadcaster, but I didn't.

I said, "Are you kidding? This guy has an awful voice."

McFarlane was relentless, though, and he decided to give him an audition. Dick was extremely nervous, but he got the job.

When he started on the air, Dick wasn't seated behind a desk. He got into the habit of leaning on his stool. Once, just before he went on the air, I grabbed the stool and took it away.

He said, "What the heck are you doing? That's my stool!"

I said, "In this business there's one thing you have to learn, and that's how to stand on your own two feet."

He got through the broadcast, and has always thanked me for removing the "soother."

Dick was creative and very organized. He could write scripts, do play-by-play, conduct interviews. When you look at Dick Irvin, you are looking at the consummate broadcaster. And he later wrote books. There was no assignment he couldn't tackle.

When the time came to replace Keith Dancy as Danny's colour man, I knew Dick was the right guy, even before we auditioned him. I'd worked with him long enough to appreciate what he had to offer. I wanted a young voice, and Dick was in his early thirties. Like Brian McFarlane in Toronto, I knew he would bring a shot of creativity to our show. I knew he would mesh well with Danny, and I knew Danny would respect him because of the Irvin pedigree (Dick's father, Dick Irvin Sr., had coached Chicago, Montreal and Toronto to the Stanley Cup finals sixteen times, winning three times with the Canadiens and once with the Leafs).

Molson, our sponsor, didn't care for Dick Irvin. They didn't like his voice, saying it was a little unusual, a bit thin, for television. But as far as I was concerned, he was the right guy for Danny Gallivan — and for me, that was the most important thing. And, of course, in the long run Irvin's voice became very recognizable, familiar and authoritative.

I wanted a hockey guy, and Dick was hockey — through and through. Danny respected Dick and knew Dick would take the heat off him — handling the replays and making all the adjustments in terms of the technical revolution the industry was going through.

The two of them were a study in contrasts. Dick was a team player; Danny wasn't. Gallivan liked to do things his way, but Irvin would listen to me and take direction. To build a championship team, you need superstars and you need checkers — but you also need to have true professionals, and both men fit that description.

Not that they didn't have their weak spots. Dick's voice was a little high-pitched and thin. But that was part of my plan — viewers knew when Danny was talking and they knew when Dick was talking. Many producers thought this way — that the two voices have to be different. Eventually, Dick's voice became instantly recognizable.

I knew that Dick would bring ideas to the table. The other thing I liked about him as a person was his style. Maybe I was naïve at the time — I was thirty-two — but I thought that when you do a show like *Hockey Night in Canada*, which was a gem, character was important. I didn't want to see my guys drunk in bars. They represented our show when they were on the road. People looked at them and immediately thought of *Hockey Night in Canada*. Dick is a very classy, good guy. He neither drank nor smoked. And he wouldn't dream of looking at another woman. He was the kind of real straight arrow I was looking for. The model for future hiring, I might add.

I always said that there were three rules for being a good broadcaster, and they were: (1) preparation; (2) preparation; and (3) preparation. And nobody was better prepared than Dick. He had something on everybody who was involved in the game he was broad-casting.

Dick also had a reverence for the game. If anything drives him crazy, it's the clutching and grabbing and holding. If he bemoans anything, it's how the game has deteriorated.

Of all the guys I ever worked with, Dick Irvin is the guy I respect the most. He never let me down. He was from Regina, as was my first wife. In fact, he was in my wedding party, and our wives, Janet Mellanby and Wilma Irvin, became close friends. I regret now that both are gone.

The one thing he never forgave me for was the fact that I used to make him go into the dressing room of the team that won the Stanley Cup. I did it because he was so good at recognizing the players. Of course, it was ironic that he doesn't drink, yet here were all the players spraying champagne all over the room.

Every year, he'd say, "I don't want to do that this year."

And every year I'd make him do it.

What can I say? He was so good at it, so prepared. He'd know every player without needing the cue cards.

One thing I think I regret about Dick's career is that, unlike Brian McFarlane or Dan Kelly, he never got a shot at the American market, except as an occasional between-periods guest when I was at NBC. I guess it was because he was very uniquely Canadian.

* * *

In 1984, during the off-season, I went to Prince Edward Island, in part to attend a golf tournament, but also to have a talk with Danny, who was making it known that he was going to retire. My job was to talk him out of it. He had missed a couple of games the season before, withdrawing from the Challenge Cup because of a bad throat, but he had been *the* voice of the Canadiens through more than 1,800 games. I think he was seventy at the time, but that didn't matter; he was still our biggest star.

We sat on the bluffs at his cottage, and I told him, "Danny, we don't care about age." I added, "I want you here as long as I'm here."

He said, "Ralph, I can't see the ice … I'm done." He had glaucoma in one eye and, he said, "My work is deteriorating. I can't see out of my right eye."

We sat there and cried, the both of us.

I put my arm around him and he said, "I don't want anybody to know."

I went to Molson, and took Frank Selke with me because Frank was always my confidant, and they made Danny their ambassador. He travelled across Canada and spoke at different functions, such as minor hockey banquets. He absolutely loved this role, especially if golf was involved.

After I left *Hockey Night*, I went on to work on the Winter Olympics in Calgary, and Danny was the main speaker at a celebrity golf tournament in Red Deer, Alberta. He got up to speak — and you have to remember, he and I had had a lot of arguments. (I can't say I had that sort of a relationship with the other talent.)

Danny got up and said, "There is a man in this room who is doing the Olympics in Alberta, and I want to introduce him. He's my former boss, Ralph Mellanby. He is the consummate television professional."

It was one of the biggest thrills of my life.

Danny passed away in 1993. One of the tasks I'm proudest of is serving on the board of directors of the Danny Gallivan Scholarship Fund, which gives young men and women the opportunity to continue their education.

* * *

As far as Dick is concerned, I was proud to nominate him for his Sports Media Canada Lifetime Achievement Award. We are still in touch every few weeks and will celebrate his fortieth anniversary with *Hockey Night in Canada*.

Danny and Dick — both in the Hockey Hall of Fame — were the greatest broadcast team in hockey history.

Chapter 4

THE COMPLETE BROADCASTER DAN KELLY

> "Dan Kelly is the greatest hockey broadcaster in USA history." — Ralph Mellanby on Kelly's induction into the Hockey Hall of Fame

It was a huge mistake on the part of Len Casey, the new head of sports at the CBC, but it turned out to be a lucky break for me. Dan Kelly was calling play-by-play on the CBC's Canadian Football League telecasts and was great at it. But at his first meeting with his new boss, Casey told him, "You're doing a good job calling football, but I don't think I can keep you on network sports."

"Why not?" Kelly wondered.

"Can you act? Can you sing?"

"No."

"Well, you can't work for the CBC."

"Why not?"

"Acting, singing … that's show business. You've never done anything like that, so how can you be a great announcer on football?"

Kelly was fired from the CFL broadcasts. What a reason to get rid of such a rich talent!

At the same time, we were looking for a host to replace Frank Selke on the Montreal Canadiens games. It was my second season as executive producer of *Hockey Night in Canada*, and Selke was leaving us to become general manager of the Oakland Seals. I loved Dan's work, and I was looking for a whole new crew in Montreal. To me, Dan Kelly had great potential, and it didn't hurt matters that he was a good-looking young man. So I suggested he audition for the job. He was interested, but he wasn't really sure he was the right choice.

"I'm not a host," Kelly pouted. "I'm a play-by-play man!"

"You can do play-by-play for us on radio," I told him, "but the TV job available is as host." And so he auditioned.

We had a number of other talented guys try out for the job, including Alex Trebek, who went on to fame as host of the television game show *Jeopardy!* In the end, I had quite a decision to make. Kelly was good during his audition, as I knew he would be, but others were better. Still, I had a gut feeling about Danny. Finally, I brought Kelly and Dick Irvin into my office and said, "You two guys are the finalists. I'll tell you what: I'm going to hire you both."

Dick said, "Wonderful. My dream job has finally come true."

Dan said, "How much does it pay?"

I laughed to myself. That was Dan — strictly upfront.

Danny was aggressive; he wanted to change the show. On my first visit to Ottawa, we decided to take advantage of being there by doing an intermission feature with Dan's best pal, Ralph Backstrom of the Canadiens. After filming, we were on our way back into town when Dan piped up and said, "I don't want to be the host of the show if we can't show fights." (Our policy at the time was to swing the cameras away from a fight.) I actually admired that he would take a stance on how he wanted to present *Hockey Night in Canada* as host. Of course, I was still the boss, but it is comforting to know that your talent isn't afraid to speak up.

The next year, we showed the fights.

However, it was still the policy of *Hockey Night in Canada* never to replay fights. The sponsors — Imperial Oil and Molson — didn't want them replayed. But on the night of April 4, 1968, Ted Green of the Boston Bruins and John Ferguson of the Montreal Canadiens engaged in a doozy of a battle that proved to be a key moment in the game and the series, which Montreal ultimately swept. That same night, CBC News had its hands full, covering both the Liberal leadership convention at which Pierre Trudeau was named prime minister of Canada and the assassination of the Reverend Dr. Martin Luther King Jr. in Memphis.

The Green–Ferguson bout took place at the eight-minute mark of the first period, and we weren't yet on the air. Ferguson prevailed, and without a doubt, it changed the character of the game — the Bruins seemed deflated, while the Canadiens grew visibly bolder. Kelly came up to me all excited and announced, "This is it. This is it, kid. When we hit the air, we've got to replay that fight."

I looked at him and said, "You're right. We've got to show it."

So, for the first time on *Hockey Night in Canada*, that is exactly what we did. In doing so, I broke the rules, and I knew I would hear about it.

I said to Kelly, "It's my job on the line, but let's go for it."

Kelly said, "It's your ass, not mine. Thank God."

Kelly was brilliant. We were in the first intermission when the CBC picked up the game, and Kelly said, "Normally, this is not the kind of thing you would see on *Hockey Night in Canada*, but this is a TV first. There were no goals in the first period, but we're going to show you the Ferguson–Green fight, as it might be a key moment in the series."

And away we went — into television history — together.

I was in the truck, gulping hard as the fight went out over the air. It was not long before I got raked over the coals.

A call came into the truck, and it was my boss.

"What the fuck is going on?"

"We'll talk about it tomorrow," I replied, and hung up the phone. I thought surely I'd be fired, but I wasn't.

As it happened, all the papers, including *The Globe and Mail*, praised our coverage and the change in policy. Our show now had credibility. Whether you like fighting in hockey or not, there is no denying that, as a form of intimidation, it can have a significant influence over the outcome of games. It was our show's significant move forward into television journalism.

Dan would have been the absolute star of *Hockey Night in Canada* had he elected to remain with the show, instead of moving to St. Louis after just one year, where he became the legendary voice of the Blues. Kelly was a great friend of Scotty Bowman's from their Ottawa days and always idolized him. Dan received great insights and guidance from hockey's greatest coach, and I feel this really helped his work. And I'm certain that Bowman, who was coach and general manager of the Blues, had a great deal to do with Dan getting the offer.

After that first year, I got a call from Kelly, who told me KMOX (the CBS affiliate) in St. Louis was interested in hiring him. The funny thing is, I already knew they were going to hire him. CBS had gotten the U.S. rights to cover the NHL, and I knew they wanted Kelly because he could do everything. I also knew I would be directing hockey for them in their first year, 1969. So I was on the inside, but I could not tell Danny because doing so would violate a confidentiality agreement with CBS.

"Well," he said to me, "they're after me at KMOX to do sports." He didn't know yet that they wanted him to call the action for hockey games. He thought he'd be doing just football and baseball ... and making a pile of money in the process.

I said, "Dan, you've got to take the job in St. Louis."

"But I love hockey and I know I'm going to replace Danny Gallivan. Just give me the same money they have offered me."

He would have succeeded Gallivan, too. Had he stayed, he would have eventually become the new voice of the Montreal Canadiens.

"Danny," I responded, "you've got to do it. It's going to be the biggest thing for you, ever. CBS is going to get hockey and I think you could do network hockey."

Kelly said, "No way!"

I knew CBS was going to get Kelly away from me one way or another, but I couldn't be totally frank with him.

"I can't compete with their offer," I told him. "You'd better take the job."

The next week he called me and said, "That's it. I took the job. I'm resigning."

I said, "I know, and you're also going to do CBS hockey."

We laughed, and he said, "You son of a bitch! You knew all along."

Kelly's departure turned out to be Bob Cole's big break. I know Cole would not have had a chance to succeed Gallivan and Hewitt had Kelly not moved to St. Louis and the Blues.

We never worked together after that, but we did see each other on occasion, usually in New York. We were pals. We went to see the *Ed Sullivan Show* together, went to Broadway shows. I got to know and really like both Dan and his wife, Fran. I generally liked to get to know my broadcasters away from the arena. I would visit Dan in Ottawa and we'd golf — and believe me, golfing with Dan (a lefty) was a true adventure.

Once, in Ottawa, I was really beating him badly.

He said, "Hey, Ralph, can you fight?"

I said, "You're damned right I can fight."

He said, "That's good, because you sure as hell can't golf."

I said, "Danny, look at the scoreboard."

To give you a real insight into Kelly's love of golf, at the first *Hockey Night in Canada* golf tournament in Montreal, I teamed with Dan, Dick Irvin and Danny Gallivan. We were the last foursome off the tee, and what an experience it was. Kelly was, as usual, all over the first hole — and I mean that literally. He was everywhere; must have shot a twelve.

When we finished the hole, I said, "Scores?"

Irvin: "Par."

Gallivan: "Bogey."

Mellanby: "Bogey."

Kelly: "There's nobody behind us; I want to start again."

I said, "Danny, it's a tournament. You can't."

"I won't win anyway," Dan said. "I'm going back to the first tee."

And off he went — with *my* golf cart.

When he finally caught up to us on the second hole — with me walking — he said, "Give me a bogey on the first hole."

I looked at Irvin, who smiled and said, "Well, as a golfer and as an announcer, he has a great imagination."

Oh, Kelly didn't win the tournament, but boy did we have fun!

Dan liked things his way, and he was famous for being opinionated. He'd argue with his colour guys on the air. It was belligerent, but he liked to make his point. He had a very analytical mind. His colour man would make a comment and Dan would pipe up and say, "I'm not so sure about that." He wasn't trying to show up his partner, but he loved controversy and he really knew the game. Danny was a true Irishman — up front and always willing to speak his mind, on the air or off.

It was the same in terms of his dealings with me, even after he left us. We'd bump into each other and he'd say, "I don't like what you guys are doing at *Hockey Night in Canada*." Or, "I didn't really care for that feature you guys are running." Or, "I hate Peter Puck!"

That said, he was also a champion eater. He knew all the great restaurants around the league. He was famous for his enormous appetite and he was always fun to go out with. Once, at Mama Leona Pizzeria & Italian Restaurant in New York (where they served the food in large buckets), he actually set an NHL record by asking for seconds.

He was a loyal friend. Once, while he was working for CBS, he walked into the media room and overheard my guys complaining about me.

All he could hear was, "Mellanby this ... Mellanby that," and "Mellanby has lost it."

He walked over to them and said, "How many Emmys have you won? Well, how many? Mellanby has won five!"

That shut them up in a hurry.

I spoke with Dan two weeks before he died of cancer in February 1989.

"Ralph, I have great faith. I am content," he told me.

The last thing he mentioned was about his sons, who were both into hockey broadcasting.

"Don't worry," he assured me. "They are going to be great, but maybe not as great as their old man."

Like their father, both Dan Jr. and his brother John have become excellent NHL broadcasters, and I know Danny would have been proud of their work.

Dan Kelly was the complete broadcaster, one who prided himself on his voice and his accuracy. He never made a mistake. He worked for CBS, CTV and several other networks and was always the first choice of American networks to do the Stanley Cup final, but he was most famous as the voice of the Blues. When my son, Scott, played for the Blues, I used to love going to the games and seeing his banner (with the Irish shamrock) hanging from the rafters.

I loved Dan Kelly and miss him ... in the restaurant ... in the media room ... on the golf course. And, of course, on the air — especially on the air.

Chapter 5

THE VOICE OF HOCKEY BOB COLE

> "They're going home ... they're going home. We
> went to Russia and took it all, but now they're going
> home." — Bob Cole, as the Soviets left the ice at the
> Philadelphia Spectrum during a heated exhibition
> game against the Flyers

I take a lot of pride in the broadcasters I hired to call the action on *Hockey Night in Canada*. Most of them, I found. Bob Cole, however, found me.

I got a call at my office one day in 1968 — I always used to answer my own phone back then — and the voice on the other end (and what a voice it was) said, "Hi, it's Bob Cole from Newfoundland."

"Who?"

Bob was working for the CBC in Newfoundland, covering sports and hosting a quiz show, but I didn't know who he was.

"Alan Gilroy [the head of CBC Radio sports] suggested I call you because I am interested in auditioning for *Hockey Night in Canada* on radio."

I'm not really sure why, but I instantly had a good feeling about Bob. The Stanley Cup finals were in full swing and the Canadiens were playing the Bruins. I admired Cole's courage to call me and told him that, if he paid his own way to Montreal and arranged to work with an engineer, I'd find him a spot in the gondola where he could record the action for his audition tape.

Bob recalls that he couldn't believe it. Here he was, talking immediately to the executive producer of Canada's number one show.

"You mean, just come and do it?" he said.

I told him I wasn't guaranteeing anything, but I'd get him passes for the game and secure a spot in the booth for them. The rest was up to him. The reality was that this was a hugely busy time of year, so I didn't have the time to cater to him. Sure enough, Bob and his guys made their way to the game. He brought in his own crew and equipment and made the tape.

I didn't hear from him for the longest time — at least a few weeks. Then I received the tape, along with a letter telling me how appreciative he was for my having allowed him to do the game, especially during the finals. I liked what I heard on the tape and said, "This guy is good — and he's different. He has a great hockey voice for radio." I wasn't even thinking about television.

I tried out the tape on my producers and they liked him.

That summer, I flew him back to Montreal and spent a morning with him. I told him upfront that we could only use him on a sporadic basis and that, if he did well, I'd increase his assignments. We had lost Dan Kelly to the United States, so that opened up a slot on our Sunday radio shows. And later, when Danny Gallivan decided he didn't want to do radio anymore, I chose to hire Cole to replace him on the Montreal broadcasts.

Bob was good from the get-go. He made his mark immediately, and everybody liked him. As was my custom as executive producer, I started to socialize a little bit with Bob, trying to get to know him better. I'd visit him and his family in Newfoundland and we'd play a little golf and tennis. I liked him as a person and loved the way he called the games. That said, he could occasionally be a little difficult to deal with.

I feel that, when the Summit Series between Canada and the Soviet Union took place in 1972, two media stars were born: Howie Meeker on television and Bob Cole in the radio booth. Bob was the first guy I really felt I could mould to call the games the way I felt they should be called. I wanted change, and Bob was teachable; he would listen to instruction. I got him to bring the colour man into play more often while the play was in progress. That was a first. Bob and I worked out a system of hand signals: when the colour man wanted to make a point, he would signal Bob, who would give him the floor. The reason why we elected to use hand signals was because Bob hated to be touched while he was working. With other announcers, I had developed a touch system to bring in the analyst ... but Bob would have no part of that.

Shortly after Bob made the transition from radio to television, he showed up one day wearing a toupee. I was shocked.

"You don't need that," I told him.

"I'm trying to look good for TV," he said.

"No, no," I insisted. "You *really* don't need that."

After a few weeks, he relented and took it off. First he had no hair, then he had hair, then he returned to having no hair. I told him he looked much better *au naturel*.

* * *

I used to tell my guys, and the sponsors, too, that one of the strengths of *Hockey Night in Canada* was the fact that our announcers came from all over Canada. We were a coast-to-coast broadcast, if you will. Eventually, our play callers were Jim Robson from British Columbia, Cole from Newfoundland, Gallivan from the Maritimes, the Hewitts from Toronto, Don Wittman from Manitoba, Dick Irvin from Saskatchewan and Brian McFarlane from the Ottawa Valley.

I was often asked why Bob Cole didn't move to Toronto, to be more centrally located, and I told people that is not what we wanted. We wanted him in Newfoundland. I felt that *Hockey Night* was Canada's show, and it was important to have representation from all across the country. You have to pay for their travel, but so what? I used to tell the sponsors it served us well — that's why it's called

Hockey Night in Canada, not *Hockey Night in Toronto.*

I loved Bob's passion and emotion. He put something new into the game broadcasts. Bob was opinionated, but he had a very good sense of the show and what we wanted. His best asset was his sense of the dramatic. It was also a plus for *HNiC* that he wasn't identified with a particular team — Gallivan was Montreal and the Hewitts were Toronto, but Cole was like a free agent who bounced from club to club, game to game. He was our first real national announcer. He had a wonderful relationship with his first colour man, Mickey Redmond, whom he worked with most of the time until Harry Neale was hired.

Bob also had the best hockey voice — it matched the game. It was different, indeed, but it made people take notice.

He was also something of an eccentric. He smoked and always used a long cigarette holder. And like Cherry, his dress — off-air — was a little different. He'd call the games, if you can believe this, with the belt on his pants undone. And as I mentioned, he was very uptight and absolutely hated to be touched.

"Don't touch me when I work!" he'd say to anybody who dared do so.

Sometimes the loose belt got him into trouble. More than once, when he got excited, he'd jump up and his pants would fall down. That's why we never had a female assistant director working in the booth with him.

Bob was also a little on the gullible side. Let's face it, he was a small-town boy. Once, we were at a conference with our talent — all the guys you see and hear on camera — and the gathering also included many of the sponsors. Bob got up and spoke, and some of what he said was a little on the blue side. The next day, Dave Hodge bumped into Bob and said, "Boy, with what you said last night ... I hear you're gone."

Of course, Dave was only kidding, but Bob took him quite seriously. He was on the bus to the airport with the rest of the gang and he was almost in tears. I asked him what was wrong and he said,

"Dave Hodge and the guys told me I'm going to be fired."

I immediately deduced what was going on and said, "The guys are just putting you on. Don't listen to them ... listen to me. I'm the guy who says who's fired, and you're here for a long, long time." (And he has been with *Hockey Night* for more than thirty years.)

With that, he said he was going to punch Hodge out. Once before, he had got into a physical altercation with Rick Briggs-Jude, and I reminded him that he had already been told, "Don't you ever lay a hand on one of our people again, because if you do, you *will* be fired." Bob was short, but really strong and tough as nails. Eventually the whole practical joke blew over, and Hodge was lucky to live to tell about it — Cole might have killed him.

After I left *HNiC* in 1985, Bob and I drifted apart. Truth be told, I think he was a little hurt when I left the show. I often wonder if he felt as if I betrayed him and the show. I don't know.

Some members of the press have suggested that Bob has stayed on too long. I'm not really sold on that notion, though. He may have some problems keeping up with the names of players, but since the league expanded to thirty teams, to say he is alone in that department is silly. Because Bob does all the big games — including the Stanley Cup finals and the All-Star Game — the press tends to notice his few mistakes more than others. The fact is, all the broadcasters make errors today. There are just too many players, and many of them you rarely see. Hell, you get some announcers who can't even properly pronounce the names of the players on the team they cover for an entire season.

Bob Cole is a fiercely intense, competitive person and one of the hardest-working, most completely prepared broadcasters I ever worked with. He was blessed with a great hockey voice. As a matter of record, he has, over the years, become the voice of hockey and has been deservedly honoured by the Hockey Hall of Fame. Bob ranks right up there with the greats — Danny Gallivan, Dan Kelly and Foster Hewitt — as the standards by which hockey play-by-play announcers are measured.

I am very proud of Bob because I discovered him — or, at least, he discovered me. I still love to listen to his work — his tone, tempo and passion for the game, the ebb and flow of his voice and his unique sayings. Just as Gallivan had his "cannonading" and Foster had his "He shoots! He scores!" Bob has his "I'll tell you, mister."

Yes, Bob is an original, both as a broadcaster and as a man. But thank God we passed on the hairpiece!

Chapter 6

THE HOST'S HOST
DAVE HODGE

> "I hired Dave Hodge, and eventually my son, Scott, fired him." — Ralph Mellanby on the cancellation of Hodge's contract with *Hockey Night in Canada*

Being an executive producer means having to make tough decisions. Such was the case when I decided to replace Ward Cornell as host of *Hockey Night in Canada* in Toronto. It was considered a huge change on our show.

The fact of the matter is, I really liked Ward as a person. He was my best friend on the show and we shared similar backgrounds. We were college educated and loved theatre and music, and every playoffs we'd have an Academy Awards party when we were on the road. I was the only person from *Hockey Night* to be invited to his second wedding. We were very close.

As executive producer, however, I realized the show had to take precedence over personal relationships and friendships, and I felt the Toronto broadcast looked old. The host is basically the brand of the show, and the brand looked ancient.

I had hired Dan Kelly and Dick Irvin in Montreal, so my team there was youthful — two guys in their early thirties. And I had Brian McFarlane, who was young and vital, in Toronto.

As much as it pained me, I knew Ward had to go.

This was not an easy, or popular, decision. You have to remember,

Ward Cornell had a huge following in Canada. He was something of a father figure and was popular.

Ted Hough, my boss, fought me to the death on this one, but the producers I had were young and they felt the same way as I did — we needed a young, bright guy. (I really wanted Alex Trebek, who was working for the CBC in Ottawa. Was he lucky or what?) Frank Selke, our VP of everything, backed me as usual, and he also had Hough's ear.

Word got out that the hosting job for *Hockey Night in Canada* in Toronto was open, and you can just imagine the lineup for it.

I hardly knew Dave Hodge; all I knew was that he worked for CFRB and he had done some play-by-play on junior telecasts and for the Buffalo Sabres. What I had seen, I liked. I liked his voice, his appearance and his youth. He represented the image I was looking for — even with his long hair, which was still an issue in the '60s. Also, when he did interviews on the radio, I thought he had a real journalistic bent. I have a fetish about good journalism, and he was a guy who would ask the right questions ... and the tough ones, too.

He wouldn't ask the old standbys, like "Isn't it great to be in the NHL?" or "Where did you play your junior hockey?" If I'd heard Ward Cornell ask one more player where they spent their junior careers, I think I might have dropped dead!

I didn't want to conduct the auditions because I wanted to avoid being prejudiced, so I handed the reins to my top producer, Bob Gordon, along with a good director, Cecil Brown. We held two days of auditions at CFTO in Toronto, and twelve men tried out for the job. They all taped an intro, read a news script and interviewed a player, Jim Pappin. In the end, I viewed the tapes, and Hodge's audition was the worst. He was nervous ... not the self-assured guy that I had seen on Buffalo television. Also, he didn't seem prepared. But he had the look I wanted, and I had a strong hunch that he was our man.

I went back to Bob and said, "What do you think?"

He said Don Chevrier was really good, and this guy and that guy were really good.

I told him, "I want to re-audition Hodge, but I want to be there."
The funny thing is, Dave didn't really desire the job. Or at least
he wasn't desperate to get it the way some of the other candidates
were. He didn't think he was ready. Perhaps in the future, but not
now. Understandable — nobody his age and with his inexperience
really wanted to replace an icon of Canadian television like Ward
Cornell.

When we did the second audition, I instructed him to simply,
"Do your thing ... be yourself. Don't worry about technical stuff.
Just do it. I can teach you the other stuff."

This time around, I chose Selke as the subject of the mock interview — a real pro and an intelligent man with a lot to say, someone
Hodge could play well off of.

I was right about Dave: he did a bang-up job the second time
around.

When it came time to present our potential new host to the
sponsors, I brought one tape with me: Dave Hodge. I felt that I had
my guy, and they couldn't help but buy into him.

The chain of events that led to his hiring really knocked David
out. I was in Montreal for a meeting with the sponsors, and I flew
him in, first class, from Toronto. I met him in the airport lounge, sat
with him, hired him and then sent him back on the next plane to
Toronto — first class. He couldn't believe it. But this was the jewel of
Canadian television, and we did things first class. He got his contract
and his *Hockey Night in Canada* blue jacket. A new era was upon us.

We did one dress rehearsal with him during a pre-season game,
and right from the start, he was great. Once he got the job, he
embraced it.

There was one little speed bump we had to deal with, though.
Behind my back, my boss Ted Hough, who loved Ward Cornell, gave
him six guest appearances on the show. Now Dave had to interview
Ward on the air — not once, but six times. How much pressure can
you put on a guy?

It was a stupid thing to do, and Ted shouldn't have done it

without asking, but I couldn't do anything about it because my boss was my boss. Dave just about crapped his pants when he found out about it — he was so angry. This was his big career opportunity, and now he had to remind people of the past by interviewing the guy he replaced. Can you imagine that happening today? Actually, David did a good in-depth interview with Cornell every time, and it helped the audience accept him.

Dave brought an immediate glow to *Hockey Night in Canada*. He was *Hockey Night in Canada*.

Dave was also independent. He had his way of doing things and wasn't afraid to say so. In all the years I worked on *Hockey Night*, he was the most difficult guy I had to deal with. Never mind Danny Gallivan or Don Cherry, or all of the rest of the guys combined. Dave was my biggest challenge and my greatest reward.

He was a perfectionist who thought he should be the producer of the show. His mind was so sharp that young producers (guys who are giants today, like John Shannon and Doug Beeforth) were intimidated by him. He didn't think they were as smart as he was, and you know what? He was right. He wanted to do things his way. He had strong opinions about what should be on the show and about all our intermission content. He was never wrong, and I loved working with his ideas.

He also had a thing about not meeting with guests he was going to interview. He wanted to do them dead cold. I wasn't crazy about that, but I let him have his way. That's also the way Johnny Carson worked, so I wonder if that's where he picked it up. We talked about it several times, and Dave made it clear that he really didn't want his guest to know what he was going to ask; that way he could surprise the guest with the tough questions. That's probably why Harold Ballard hated David.

Dave was by far our best interviewer. He asked tough questions, but he had a way of putting his guests at ease. He wasn't into lobbing softballs at his guests, but his delivery didn't offend them.

Much as Hodge did his own thing, he occasionally looked to

others for advice. The guy he listened to more than me on our show was Jack Dennett, his mentor. He couldn't have picked a better guy; Jack was our patriarch. I always loved Jack and tried to work him in as often as I could. Dave leaned on him a bit for historical perspective.

Whenever there was a big event — the Stanley Cup, the conference finals, the All-Star Game, the Challenge Cup, the Super Series — I went into the truck myself to produce. My producers didn't like it; they thought I was grabbing the glory and keeping the big events to myself. In truth, I did it mainly because of Dave. I really wanted to have control of him because I knew he would follow my lead.

As an example, when the Russians left the ice in Philadelphia in Super Series '76, I was in Dave's ear. I told him to go out to the hallway because I'd heard Flyers owner Ed Snider was holding the Soviets' cheque and wasn't going to give it to them unless they finished the game. Dave did as I directed. He might say after a show that he didn't agree with something like this, but I was the guy who found him and he did it, if not my way, then our way. He also knew that I would back him, no matter what; so, even if he didn't like me at times, I knew I had his respect. We both had big egos, but we also shared a passion for our show.

I guess he also thought I was as smart as he was — or at least nearly?

Dave's departure from *Hockey Night* is part of the folklore of Canadian television. It has gone down in history as the "pencil incident."

I like to say that I hired Dave and my son, Scott, fired him.

By the time of the incident (March 14, 1987), I'd left to work on the Calgary Olympics, and that night I was hosting the world leaders of sports broadcasting at Glen Sather's place in Banff, Alberta. It was a fun, easygoing evening, and a lot of the guys wanted to watch *Hockey Night in Canada*. The Calgary–Toronto game ended, and the network switched to the Philadelphia–Montreal game, where there was less than a minute remaining and the Canadiens were ahead by a goal.

Wouldn't you know it? Scott scored to tie the game, setting up overtime. The CBC went to a commercial, after which they returned to Dave, who was being told on the air that stations that had carried the Toronto feed would not see the end of the Montreal game — instead, *The National* would begin, as scheduled, at 11 o'clock. This violated the golden rule of *Hockey Night in Canada*, which was, "Don't go to an alternate telecast if you aren't planning to stay there." Hodge was already pissed because, earlier in the day, the CBC was covering the Brier, and it had taken a semifinal match off the air while it was still in progress in order to switch to coverage of the NDP convention. He later told anyone who would listen that he'd thought that was an awful network decision, too.

I didn't actually see what happened next. After all, I had all these guys sitting in the living room watching the game, so I was in the kitchen making sure everybody's drink was topped up.

When Dave got the word that he was to wrap up and intro the news, he said, "We are not able to go there…the Flyers and Canadiens have us in suspense and will remain that way until we can find out somehow who won this game or who's responsible for the way we do things here. Goodnight for *Hockey Night in Canada*." Clearly frustrated Hodge flips his pencil in the air.

I don't know how the rest of the country reacted, but I can tell you that Don MacPherson, the head of CBC Sports, who was at my party, was not impressed. He was embarrassed. Who wouldn't be, with the giants of television surrounding us — people like Roone Arledge, the head of ABC News and Sports, and David Hill, then with Australian television, who later headed Fox Sports (and is now with DirecTV)? I tried to calm MacPherson down, telling him to worry about it tomorrow. We all left the house to go to a restaurant, and by this time the guys were feeling kind of "happy" and started giving Don the business at dinner. The head of Soviet television said, "If that was my guy, I'd send him to Siberia!"

By the time we got back to my place, MacPherson was livid. He had pretty much made up his mind that Hodge was done. He never got off the phone — and never paid me for the long-distance calls!

That opened the door for Ron MacLean to take the position as national host for *Hockey Night in Canada,* and we all know how well he has succeeded.

It was an odd ending to an era. Had I been running the show in Toronto, we wouldn't have joined a game in progress unless we were going to stay with it to the end. Had I been there, Dave still might be the host today.

Hodge rebounded and went on to have a great career. He now works for TSN and is still a very fine broadcaster and journalist. I nominated Dave for the Sports Media Canada Lifetime Achievement Award, and I went to the presentation. He thanked me for taking a risk on a kid with long hair. I am very proud of my choice, and I believe he will someday be honoured by the Hockey Hall of Fame.

We had our share of disagreements and fights, but we shared this in common — our passion for *Hockey Night in Canada* and the game.

Chapter 7

MASTER OF THE TELESTRATOR HOWIE MEEKER

> "He wouldn't be half as good if he didn't have his magic pencil." — Don Cherry on Howie Meeker's use of the telestrator

I inflicted Don Cherry on an unsuspecting Canadian nation, and some people have said I found Howie Meeker under a rock. Not true: I actually found Howie *on* the Rock!

Howie enjoyed a brief but very successful career as an NHL player. He broke into the league in 1946–47 with the Toronto Maple Leafs and was the NHL's rookie of the year after scoring 27 goals and 45 points in 55 games. A small but skilled forward, Howie was third in team scoring behind a pair of future Hall of Famers, Ted Kennedy and Syl Apps, and he tied an NHL record for most goals in a game by a rookie, scoring five against the Chicago Black Hawks on January 8, 1947.

The Maple Leafs won the Stanley Cup in Meeker's first three seasons, and again in 1950–51. After retiring prematurely due to a back injury, Howie coached the Pittsburgh Hornets to an American Hockey League crown in 1954–55. He coached the Maple Leafs in 1956–57, finishing out of the playoffs with a 21–34–15 record.

After leaving the game, Howie ran a sporting goods store in St.

John's, Newfoundland, and operated hockey schools there. He loved teaching kids the finer points of the game.

One day in 1968, I got a call from Ted Darling, who was our host on *Hockey Night in Canada* in Montreal at the time. He was staying at the Mount Royal Hotel, and he said, "Guess who's in town?"

"Who?"

"Howie Meeker."

My ears perked up because, when I was a boy, I used to pretend I was Howie Meeker when we played hockey. That's what kids did when a game of hockey broke out — you'd scream out your favourite player's name and then it was game on.

"What's he here for?" I asked.

"He's here for a Canadian Sports Show. He has a sporting goods store in St. John's, Newfoundland. I think he'd be a great guest analyst for us."

At that time, we would rotate guest analysts on *Hockey Night in Canada*. One night it could be Jean Beliveau, and the next it might be Red Storey or Dickie Moore. One of our regulars was longtime Montreal sportswriter Red Fisher, and he was booked for our next telecast. It was Friday as Ted and I spoke, so I told him I'd have to call Red.

Red was agreeable to being bumped, but he still wanted the $100 fee. If I had decided against giving Red the money and he elected not to pass, Howie never would have had a television career. Howie really owes a good chunk of his career to Red.

I'd asked Ted to invite Howie to appear, and he called me back and told me Howie would love to do it. I told Ted I'd have a *Hockey Night in Canada* jacket waiting for him at the rink, but I needed to know what size he was. As Ted relayed this message, it was somehow taken as meaning I thought Howie might have put on some weight. Well, that set Howie off.

"You tell Mellanby I'm the same goddamn size I was when I played — five foot ten and 175 pounds!"

I had never met Howie prior to his first game with us. I told him that he'd be up in the booth between periods with Dick Irvin, and that Dan Kelly was the host downstairs. I gave him his briefing, and he said, "I have some opinions on the game that I'd like to get off my chest."

"Listen," I told him, "you've only got three minutes after the first period and three minutes after the second period, and I'll give you a minute and a half after the game finishes. That's our format."

"What? I can't even say hello in that much time. You've got to give me more."

I told him we'd drop the usual player interview, which would give him three minutes in the first intermission and five minutes in the second. "So you can get your message out there," I said.

Howie Meeker was clearly ready for *HNiC*. But was the hockey world ready for Howie Meeker? We would know the answer to that question very shortly. Luckily for us, his first appearance was on a Saturday night, for a game between the Montreal Canadiens and Toronto Maple Leafs, which would draw one of our biggest audiences of the year. I didn't plan it that way; it just happened. As far as I was concerned, this was to be a one-shot deal, but Howie went on the air that night and stopped the country. People had never seen anything like him, and neither had I.

He called it as he saw it. If a player made a mistake, Howie would point it out.

"Look at that idiotic play! What the heck was he thinking?"

I am certain that jaws were dropping across the nation as Howie, with his squeaky voice, drilled NHLers as if he were a six-foot-six defenceman who just received a Dear John letter in the mail.

Our intermission presentation had become a little like the movie *Groundhog Day* — the same thing over and over again. We'd air highlights — and, for the most part, we'd show the goals. Predictability drove me nuts. And, apparently, it bothered Howie, too.

"I don't want to show the goals," Meeker insisted. "I don't want to show people what happened, I want to tell them why it happened. Let's show the power play where the guy fell down in front of the net."

I always felt that was Howie's creed: not what, but why!

Howie went on and on about the National Hockey League expanding to too many teams and there not being enough talent to stock them. He was not afraid to be critical of the way the game was being played. The fact is, I happened to agree with Howie. I thought that when the league doubled in size from six teams to twelve in 1967, it opened the door for a lot of minor-leaguers to make it into the NHL. The talent became watered down.

After Howie's first appearance, I came into the office a little bit later than usual. My bosses were upset; the sponsors were upset. Nobody could believe Howie was on television criticizing superstars as if they were ankle benders. It just hadn't been done before on *Hockey Night in Canada*. I went back and reviewed the tapes, and I really didn't think anything Howie said was all that outlandish. What was everybody so worked up about?

The next thing I knew, I was getting a call from NHL president Clarence Campbell. I always got along with Mr. Campbell. If he called and started the phone conversation by saying "Ralph," I knew I was all right. He probably just wanted a small favour, or to appear on the show. But when he called and addressed me as "Mr. Mellanby," I knew I was in trouble.

You can probably guess how this conversation started. He wanted to see me immediately, and he wanted to see a tape of the game.

I set up my little portable videotape player in his office, and we watched Howie. Mr. Campbell made no bones about the fact that he was not impressed with Howie's debut.

"That is the most disgusting performance I've ever seen," Campbell steamed.

The league brass wanted to know how I, as executive producer, could put a guy like this on the air. They were used to our established pattern of using ex-NHLers who would never say a negative thing about the game or the players on the air. In fairness to those players, they were conditioned to protect the game. They never really understood the journalistic principle that controversy can be good for the game. And they definitely never said anything like "That's the most stupid pass you could ever make in the situation." Frankly, I found the status quo as boring as hell and was prepared to go to the wall for Howie Meeker. I had found my superstar — my Howard Cosell.

I knew this was a huge test for me, and I was not going to be pushed around. I knew what I wanted for *HNiC*, and I was not about to be shut down by anybody — not even the league president. I felt Howie was fantastic with his "golly gee whiz" and his "Jiminy Crickets." I loved his enthusiasm and I thought he, alone, took the show to a higher level. I also loved his message — we must sell skills!

Campbell was clearly upset, but in his heart, I think he knew I was trying to advance his league through television. He was a lawyer and he was very fair. He understood that I was trying to take *Hockey Night in Canada* into the modern ages and that, in doing so, I had the NHL's best interests at heart.

I called Howie in Newfoundland, and he was on top of the world. His status as a local celebrity was off the scale thanks to his appearance on the show.

"Everybody's complimenting me for the job I did," Howie shouted.

I told him that was great and I thanked him for coming on, but the main reason for my call was to see if he wanted to sign on as a regular.

"I'm not paying my own way back to Montreal," he snorted.

After I explained to him that *Hockey Night in Canada* would cover his travelling expenses, we had a deal. There was some concern on the part of the teams about Howie being critical of players, but I told him to just go on the air and do his thing. I assured him that I would back him, no matter who came gunning for him.

I told Howie I wanted him on the next season as a regular because, quite frankly, I had never had this kind of reaction about a colour commentator before.

The next thing I knew, Howie was banned from working in the Montreal Forum. This was back in the day when the teams ran *Hockey Night in Canada*. When I first joined *Hockey Night in Canada*, teams actually had the contractual ability to veto guests from appearing on the show. I could understand a general manager not wanting certain players to appear on television, because they belonged to the team. But each week I had to turn over a script of the show, and I would be told what could and could not be done.

After a few years, I managed to get those restrictions taken out of the contract. It was like a breath of fresh air. I always had a close working relationship with the sponsors, and I told them, "You guys are spending millions of dollars — why should we let the teams dictate how we run the show?" They agreed.

Howie got banned from different arenas every year, though he never knew about it. I never let on to him what was happening behind closed doors, and week after week, he did his thing, all the while rubbing players and team brass the wrong way. The politics back then were just awful. I had to jump through hoops to give our audience the best show I could.

Anyway, I decided that, if he couldn't get into the building in Montreal, we'd use him in Toronto. One of the biggest things Howie gave me was the fact that he was a guy who could move around. Unlike the hosts or the voices in the booth, he wasn't a Leafs guy or a Canadiens guy or a Canucks guy. He was a *Hockey Night in Canada* guy with no ties to any of the three NHL teams in Canada. He was beholden to nobody but *Hockey Night in Canada*.

And Howie became *Hockey Night in Canada*'s first great star.

Not only that, but Howie wanted to grow — that's one of the things I liked about him. He had been an NHL player, coach and general manager (briefly, for the Leafs, in 1957). He always wanted to know what we could do better. One improvement came when I started to let him pick his own replays. I gave him his own monitor and allowed him to talk to the isolation director to decide which plays he wanted to highlight during the intermissions. This had never been done before. Years later, when I produced the Toronto Blue Jays telecasts, I gave Tony Kubek the same privilege.

About seven years into Howie's television career, he got banned from the Forum yet again. So I went to Red Fisher, the great Montreal hockey writer (who also did "The Fisher Report" on *Hockey Night in Canada*), and asked him if he would do a little blurb in his column about Howie being banned from the Forum. But I told him to be sure nobody knew the tip came from me.

Red went after the story, and when he talked to Canadiens GM Irving Grundman, he was told that it wasn't true — that Howie was always welcome at the Forum. I put Howie on the next Saturday, and Grundman called me in my room.

"What the hell is going on?" he demanded. "Howie Meeker is banned from the Forum."

"That's not what it said in Red Fisher's article in the paper."

What a game! What fun!

From the get-go, I knew Howie was going to be a star; someone I could work with and work on. Finally I had a star who wasn't up in the booth — who wasn't Foster Hewitt or Danny Gallivan. I always felt the game could be better. So did Howie, and he lit up the nation.

In 1975, we introduced the telestrator to the show. Howie could show highlights and diagram things on the screen to make his point. Armed with this tool, he became even more animated, though I'll never forget the first night he tried to use it. Proudly, he told the audience, "Let me show you this new invention," and the viewers didn't have a clue about what he was talking about — he had forgotten to turn it on!

Howie wanted to teach kids how to play the game properly, and he felt he could do it during intermissions by showing them the wrong way and then the right way to make plays, using NHLers as his props — as his Xs and Os. An entire generation of hockey fans would watch each week as Howie screamed, "Stop it there! Stop it there, fellas. Now, back it up a bit."

My favourite Meekerism was, "Sid, roll that back." (Except for Howie, nobody knew who the heck Sid was — he was the director in the isolation truck rolling the tape.) And, on cue, the tape of the highlight Howie was showing would come to a halt. Thanks, Sid.

Picking his own highlights was a big deal for Howie. He'd go for the less obvious plays in a game, anything where he felt he could teach a lesson. He was like a coach teaching a nation of viewers the nuances of the game. Nobody had ever done that before, and almost overnight Howie re-established himself as a star. When NBC started broadcasting NHL games in the United States, they wanted to steal Howie away from me. I wouldn't allow it, although I did permit him the occasional guest shot with the American network when they and *Hockey Night in Canada* were covering the same game.

Howie and I had a great, long relationship, but things weren't always smooth. Howie was his own man and wouldn't be bullied by anybody. He wasn't opposed to being the bully, though.

We worked together on a show called "Howie Meeker's Pro Tips," and little did we know that all the NHL players I'd lined up to appear on the program were getting ready to walk because Howie was acting like he was a coach again. He was yelling at the players as if they didn't have a clue what they were doing. We're talking about Hall of Famers such as Darryl Sittler and Larry Robinson. Damned if they were going to be pushed around. But Howie would go up to someone like Sittler and say, "That's not the way you make a backhand pass, you idiot!"

You can imagine how that went over. The players couldn't believe their ears.

I finally made Howie understand that these guys were here to try to help teach kids. I told him to let me handle the players and he could handle the pro tips. Howie never won the players over during his time with *Hockey Night in Canada*, but he didn't care. Howie lived in a Howie Meeker world — a world where he never ever felt the players were skilled enough.

Of course, there were exceptions. Howie would never dream of criticizing a player like Bobby Orr. He'd never criticize Guy Lafleur. They were great players, and Howie acknowledged that. But he'd go after a guy like Ken Dryden all the time, and Howie didn't know a thing about goaltending.

He'd say something like, "If the puck doesn't hit him, he can't stop it!" Ken Dryden is a Hall of Fame goaltender, for heaven's sake.

But that was the way I wanted it. I wanted Howie to be insulated from the rest of the world. Early in his television career, he sat at the head table at a banquet during an NHL All-Star Game and got booed. After that, Howie didn't go to NHL banquets or hang out with NHL players.

And he never changed. He was his own man.

Howie cared more about the future of the game than his performance as a television commentator. He once told me, "Some guys were scared to say their thoughts and skirted the subject by not saying what really happened. There was nothing ever instructive or critical. I had enough other things going in my life that the money I got from *HNiC* was nothing more than holiday money. It didn't matter to me if I got fired."

That attitude would serve him well over the years.

In Howie's mind, it was Howie Meeker versus the world. Even I wasn't exempt from his barbs.

Once, I was sitting with Howie and his agent, Gerry Patterson, on his porch, and he piped up: "You know the problem with you, Mellanby? You don't know half of what I know about hockey. You never played hockey."

I looked him straight in the eye and said, "That may be true, Howie, but I know a hell of a lot about television."

Point taken!

The main thing I had to do with Howie was keep him in my domain and not allow anybody to touch him. I did the same thing with Don Cherry. I had to make sure nobody messed with him. I told him to do what I told him to do. Follow the producer, follow the director, but don't let them tell him how to perform or what his act was.

During the 1972 Summit Series between the Canadian and Soviet teams, Howie was the only "expert" who picked the Russians to win the series. Everybody thought the NHL stars would trample the Soviet Union, exposing them as rank amateurs. But as we found out, Russian hockey players were not only great athletes, they knew how to play the game. They trained harder than NHLers did; they were determined and dedicated. They were not intimidated, and they had better skills than the Canadian pros.

Howie went on national television and declared that the Russians would win the eight-game series. He said the NHL players simply didn't have the skills to beat the Russians. As he went through the highlights throughout the series, he showed a shocked nation exactly how good the Soviets were and how well-coached they were. That made him a superstar. Prior to the Summit Series, Howie's credibility had always been in question. Sure, he won the Calder Trophy as the NHL's top rookie. Sure he coached in the NHL. But to a lot of people, he was nothing but an old guy with a beef.

After the '72 series, no one questioned him again. He was the one guy who dared suggest the Russians had what it took to beat the best NHLers. And even though Canada squeaked through with a victory in Game 8 to take the series, Howie had made his point. All you have to do is look at how Canadian hockey players trained and how the NHL changed after the Summit Series. Suddenly, we were using a lot of the techniques the Russians used.

Howie never said, "I told you so." But when he showed Russians dangling with the puck during the highlights, he'd say, "See what they do — that's the way hockey should be played."

He was a Canadian through and through, but he loved the skill and the creativity the Soviets brought to the table. I believe the influence of the Summit Series led to the great Oilers and Canadiens teams of the 1970s and '80s.

After I left the show in 1985, I thought Howie started to play up too much of the fact he was Howie Meeker. There were too many "golly gee whizzes." He started to become a caricature of himself, and I told him as much. Frankly, I think that is what ended his career. In the seventeen years Howie and I worked together, I thought he showed a lot of humanity and a lot of himself on the air. But by the end of his run on *Hockey Night*, he had started to portray Howie

Meeker instead of just being Howie Meeker.

That said, I thought that Howie was betrayed by *Hockey Night in Canada*. I felt he was still relevant and had a following, but the show decided to commit entirely to Don Cherry. Perhaps it was inevitable; Don was becoming a star in his own right, and he and Howie were like oil and water.

I was long gone by then, but I don't think they should have dumped him the way they did. They didn't actually fire him, they just phased him out. They didn't even bother to call Howie to let him in on their plans, which I thought was a bush-league way of handling things. Howie was one of the superstars of the show and he deserved more respect. Howie was an icon, but he wasn't treated like one. The good news is that he went on to work with TSN, and I was thrilled when Howie was inducted into the Hockey Hall of Fame in 1998 in the broadcasting category. He deserved it. But being on TSN wasn't like being on *Hockey Night*.

Howie turned the country's attitude toward the future. He was a great visionary. We can see in retrospect what happened to hockey in Canada. Way back then, he'd say, our game was eroding. He said we taught in a defensive, "hook and hold" way — in a cheating way. "We're not coaching right, dammit! We need to teach the kids skills."

I think Howie Meeker is one of the greatest Canadians who ever lived. He tried to enlist in the air force when he was eighteen, but he was rejected. So he went to the army engineering corps, and they took him. He was shipped to England, and during manoeuvres, a live grenade went off right next to him. He survived the blast but nearly lost his legs. He battled his way back into shape. Howie fought all his life. He served as a Member of Parliament in the early 1950s, something he didn't really want to do. George Drew, the fourteenth premier of Ontario, called Howie personally, and when Howie told him he wasn't interested in being a politician, he said, "You've got to serve."

When you say that to Howie Meeker, he serves.

Howie never really mixed with the others on *Hockey Night in*

Canada. He came in, did his job, shocked the nation, then went home. To me, he was the ultimate pro.

Howie's greatest attribute when we worked together was his passion for the game of hockey. But in his mind, passion without skill equalled failure.

He preferred skill *with* passion.

It is no surprise to me that a recently compiled list of the 100 most important books in Canadian history included only one sports book: *Howie Meeker's Hockey Basics.*

Chapter 8

THE SHARP-DRESSED MAN DON CHERRY

> "I hear you hired Cherry? Do you know what you're doing? He'll getcha. He'll getcha." — Harry Sinden to Ralph Mellanby upon hearing that Don Cherry had been hired full-time by *Hockey Night in Canada*

Our philosophy at *Hockey Night in Canada* was to always stay ahead of the game. We were happy with Howie Meeker, but I always wanted to introduce something new in the playoffs, particularly for the finals. I think fans grew to expect that from *Hockey Night in Canada*.

The year before I brought Cherry in, I hired Chico Resch of the New York Islanders and Lou Nanne of the Minnesota North Stars because I wanted to have the perspectives of a goalie and a general manager. We had a panel discussion on every game broadcast during the finals, and I thought things went well.

But I remained on the lookout for talent to help boost the show, and did we ever score big-time with Cherry.

I'd like to say I knew from the outset that Don would develop into a superstar, but that would be a lie. As much as I was aware of his high profile, which is one of the things that attracted me to him in the first place, I had no idea he would grow to become Canada's greatest television star.

Don had a reputation for being quite the showman when he coached the Boston Bruins. He was animated and he loved the spotlight. The same couldn't be said about most National Hockey League coaches, who tended to stand resolutely behind the bench, getting emotional only occasionally when a call went against their team.

Don could never be accused of showing a staid demeanour. Some nights, it seemed as if he cared as much about how he looked as he did about his team's play. Don's wardrobe — his fancy suits, high collars and loud ties — became his calling card. And with each passing year his suits grew more and more flamboyant. One night he'd show up in a bright purple suit, and the next in a black pinstriped outfit with a gangster's fedora. A cream-coloured suit with a bold pattern of bright red flowers was one of his favourites. (In its annual summer publication in 2004, *The Hockey News* devoted an entire article to Don and his wild wear.) Win or lose, Cherry was always the quintessential sharp-dressed man. And we needed someone who would keep the viewers' attention during the intermission. Don was my man ... in spite of his tailor.

Clearly, Don had star appeal. The Bruins had superstars such as Bobby Orr and Phil Esposito, but everywhere I went, all people ever talked about was Don. Years later, the cover of *The Hockey News's* yearbook featured not one of the NHL's many superstars, but Don Cherry.

When the photographer suggested a couple of poses for Don, he scoffed.

"Take a picture of this," he said, as he thrust his chest forward and offered up his best James Bond pose. "I know what the fans want."

Don is Bobby Orr's biggest fan. If you say anything negative about Orr to Don Cherry, you had better be prepared to drop the gloves.

When the Bruins decided to hold Bobby Orr Night on an evening when they were playing an exhibition game against the Russians, Don fumed, threatening not to dress any of his good players for the game. Bruins general manager Harry Sinden went nuts because he knew it was a big deal for both the NHL and for *Hockey Night in Canada* and felt that Cherry was embarrassing the organization. But Don felt the organization was embarrassing Orr.

I went to Don and asked what the hell was going on.

"This is an insult to Bobby," he spit. "To play against those bloody Russians. We're having Bobby Orr Night and they put us against the Russians? That's ridiculous!"

When European players began filtering into the NHL, Don made no bones about the fact that he didn't like it. Don, who loved to study history, felt many were our enemies. But the biggest problem Don had with Europeans was the fact that they were taking jobs from Canadian players on Canadian teams.

When you spend nearly two decades in the minors, hanging on to your career by the skin of your teeth — a stitch here, a broken bone there from oblivion — you develop survival instincts. Cherry felt the majority of Europeans who joined the NHL were soft, and it irked him that "good Canadian boys" were being buried in the minors while Europeans were parachuted into big-league jobs.

Don didn't give a damn about political correctness, either. That was clear just about every time he opened his mouth. He said what was on his mind, which endeared him to me, though it ruffled the feathers of the CBC brass. His first partner on "Coach's Corner," Dave Hodge, considered himself a journalist and really didn't have much use for Don's act. Hodge felt it wasn't intellectual enough, that Don was too common and brought the show down. The two never developed a relationship. Don got along better with his second host, the pun-spewing Ron MacLean, but they've never really grown close, either. Their personalities are different — I thought Don was a cold beer on a hot day, while MacLean was vintage champagne. And there have been many times when Don felt MacLean was trying to upstage him, which he doesn't like a bit.

Don called me once to complain about MacLean making jokes and taking up his time.

I told him, "Take Ron aside and tell him you're going to punch him in the nose!"

That's exactly what Don did.

Don didn't mingle with the other announcers who worked on

Hockey Night in Canada. He liked the technicians, the operators ... the little guys. The only big-name person he grew close to in the early years was play-by-play announcer Bob Cole. For some strange reason, he and Bob had a great relationship. I never got in the way of it, but I never truly understood it.

He and Bob would go out for a few beers — or "pops," as Cherry likes to call them — after each Saturday-night game. Bob flew in to Toronto from Newfoundland each Friday for the games, while Don would make the trip in from Kingston, Ontario. They would both stay at the Westbury Hotel, and they always stayed in the same rooms, right beside each other.

At the end of the night, they would retire to the hotel for a few drinks, talking endlessly about hockey, and they found a place in an alcove over each of their doors to stash their bottles so that they would be there when they returned the following week. One time I went to the hotel with a pal of mine, Ron Harrison, during the afternoon and took their bottles, just for a joke. The people who worked on *Hockey Night in Canada* were like a team and we'd pull pranks on one another. Well, they got back to their rooms and were about to sit down and solve the problems of the hockey world with a nightcap, but when they reached for their bottles, they were gone.

Boy, were they ever pissed off!

Don and I had a great relationship. Sure, we argued and had occasional disagreements, but I wasn't scared of him and he wasn't scared of me. I wanted him to go on the air and talk about substantive things, about the hockey issues of the day. I didn't care about the "chicken Swedes" or who he thought was a pansy because they chose to wear a visor. I wanted meatier stuff — things like, are the referees really intimidated by the league's chief ref? We had some great stuff.

As popular as Don was with fans (he ranked seventh in the CBC's poll of the greatest Canadians of all time, one up on fellow Kingstonian Sir John A. Macdonald and three ahead of Wayne Gretzky), he, like Howie Meeker, didn't win over all the players, some of whom felt he was picking on them in front of a national audience. In their defence, some of the players he criticized from his pulpit on Saturday night would scoff at his playing career.

Don played a grand total of one NHL game: a playoff game in 1955. He likes to joke that, when he was a kid, he prayed to God to become a professional hockey player.

"I guess I forgot to mention I wanted to play in the NHL," he says.

Don was a career minor-leaguer whose travels took him to such places as Hershey, Springfield, Trois-Rivières, Kitchener-Waterloo, Spokane, Rochester, Tulsa and Vancouver. Upon retiring as a player, Don worked in construction and then as a car salesman, but he missed the game. Besides, selling cars was absolutely no fun at all after the lifetime of thrills and spills that came with playing professional hockey.

Two years after retiring, he decided civilian life just wasn't for him and rejoined the Rochester Americans, but lasted just nineteen more games as a player before he was invited to take over as the team's coach. Don's ability as a player may not have been enough to get him to the "show" on a permanent basis, but his work behind the bench was. Players and fans alike loved him, even if management didn't. Though he was technically a part of the team's management, he always related better to the players than the "suits," which never sat well with his employers. Shortly after being named top rookie coach in the AHL, he was dismissed because management felt he was simply too close to his players. But when the fans cried foul, he was rehired.

The Bruins hired Don in 1974. They were a strong team, led by the legendary Orr and super-scorer Esposito. Don loved his players, and if you judge by the results, the players loved him right back. Boston finished 40–26–14 in his initial season, then went on to capture four straight division championships, making it to the Stanley Cup finals in 1976–77 and 1977–78.

Without question, the most memorable moment of his tenure with the Bruins occurred in Montreal during the 1979 semifinals, when his team was caught with too many men on the ice. The Canadiens went on score on the ensuing power play and won the series (and, in the next series, the Stanley Cup), though many felt the Bruins were the stronger team. To this day, a shot of Cherry, standing atop the bench, defiantly acknowledging the jeers of the Forum crowd, is featured in the intro to his "Coach's Corner" segments on *HNiC.*

Don was always at odds with his boss, Harry Sinden. When a player Sinden didn't care for did something good in the game, Don would look up to where Harry was sitting and bow or put his hands on his hips as if to say, "I told you so." You can't really blame Harry for being upset: Don was showing up his boss in public. Cherry was dismissed after that playoff. He re-emerged in Colorado and suffered through a dismal season, and that was it for his big-league coaching career.

Always one to look for a laugh, Don used to brag that when he walked across the ice in Boston he could raise his hand high in the air with his index finger pointing to the sky, to show the fans what place his team was in the standings. But in Colorado, he said, "I could show the fans both hands and both feet and I still needed to pull my pants down to show them where we stood."

I really saw a different side of Don during that series against the Canadiens.

He was very critical of television, especially *Hockey Night in Canada*, because we never replayed fights. And if there's one thing Don likes, it's a good scrap, particularly if his guy wins.

I'd learned from a child psychologist that replaying fights was bad because the replay made them seem unreal to kids, like a cartoon. That's all we needed: to be perceived as promoting violence by showing fights in slow motion. We would show the original fight in real time, because it happened, but we would never replay it.

The '77–78 season was the one in which Stan Jonathan, Boston's tough little guy (a five-foot-seven, 175-pound pit bull), beat the daylights out of Montreal enforcer Pierre Bouchard, who stood six foot two and weighed 205 pounds. One of the more memorable bouts in NHL history, it was a bloody, one-sided battle that spelled the end of Bouchard's career in Montreal.

The next time the teams played, at the Montreal Forum, another fight broke out, and this time the Bruins' player lost. The next thing I knew, there was somebody standing behind me with a hold on my shirt. Don had come blasting into my control room, about 150 feet from the Bruins' bench, screaming, "I guess you're going to replay that one, eh?"

He kept yelling and screaming at me, and all the while I was thinking to myself, if he's here, who's running the Bruins' bench? I looked up, and on a monitor I could see Don's thirteen-year-old son Tim, the team's stick boy, standing alone on the bench.

I looked Don straight in the eye and said, "Don, we don't replay any fights."

He left.

I always tell people that, from that moment on, I knew Don wanted to be on television.

For the 1980 playoffs, I wanted to bring aboard a coach who had been there, in the trenches. But I didn't want somebody from ten years ago — or thirty years ago, like Howie. I wanted a coach who knew the players in the league and whose team had just played against them. So I called Don to see if he wanted to come and work with us.

"What'll I do?" he wondered.

"All I want to know is what the coaches are thinking and what they are telling their players in all situations."

"Do I have to wear that dumb *Hockey Night in Canada* jacket?"

"Nope. You wear whatever you want. I want your personality. Just be yourself — talk like you're talking to the fans."

I like to give labels to segments, and that's when I came up with "Coach's Corner." Don made an impact right from the get-go. He was outspoken and didn't care who he offended. With Don, what you see is what you get. Nobody could play Don Cherry. He's an original. He's not educated, not in the traditional sense, but don't ever try to play him for a fool: he's very intelligent. And he's quick on his feet.

When the finals ended, with the New York Islanders winning their first of four straight Stanley Cups, nobody talked about the Islanders. They just wanted to talk about Don. I made a fateful decision — fateful, that is, for an unsuspecting Canadian television public.

I told Don, "If you don't get a coaching job, give me a call. I'd love to have you come work for me."

Don was finished in Colorado, but Toronto Maple Leafs owner Harold Ballard told me he was going to hire him. So it never really dawned on me that Don and I would work together in the near future. Ballard was one of the more colourful characters in NHL history, and I think, on some level, he related to the free-spirited Cherry. It was as if they were kindred spirits. They were both outspoken, dressed outlandishly and didn't give a damn about what others thought about them.

Ballard told me he thought Cherry was funny. Over the years, I would ask Harold why Cherry wasn't coaching his team, and he'd say, "You just wait — he will be." But it never came to pass.

Years later, I found out that Don had been blackballed by many GMs, especially the guys with influence.

The next season rolled around and my phone rang. It was Don. "Well, I don't have a job. You gave me your word."

I don't exactly remember giving him my word, but I did feel he had made a good impression on the fans during the previous year's playoffs, and I just had a feeling we could go places together.

I thought to myself, now I've got Meeker *and* Cherry. Talk about a dynamic duo. I'll put one on one week and the other the next week and drive people crazy. I couldn't help but smile to myself. One guy would tell the kids how to play the game with finesse and the other would advise them to beat the hell out of their opponents. One wanted kids to play the game with their heads; the other said it was heart that mattered most. Half the audience would love Meeker and hate Cherry; half would want to slash Howie in the kneecaps and bow at the altar of Don.

I started out in that direction, but eventually I changed things up because, with the NHL's absorption of four World Hockey Association teams, we were carrying more games, regional and national. And, much as I loved Howie, Don was definitely developing a cult following. People hated it when he wasn't on. Even those who said that they couldn't stand Don, or what he stood for, waited breathlessly during the first commercial break following the first period to hear what he had to say.

I made up my mind early that too much of Don was a bad thing. And I can honestly say I was 100 percent wrong! Unfortunately, the CBC still follows the same thought pattern, and I think they — we — make a huge mistake. You don't tell Frank Sinatra he can only sing one song; you want the entire performance.

I put him on during the first period and occasionally after the game. He'd have to stick around for the second and third periods, and that kind of bugged him, but I really felt he was having a positive impact on the show.

As I expected, Don got barred from the Montreal Forum right away. And he wasn't very popular in many other arenas, either. Even Sinden, Don's old boss and nemesis in Boston, called me and said, "Why do you have that idiot on TV?"

Of course, even though Harry and I had had a close relationship dating back to before the 1972 Summit Series, I took his perspective with a grain of salt. Don and Harry were mortal enemies who couldn't stand the sight of each other. Neither could really offer an objective opinion on the other.

The bans didn't turn out to be much of an obstacle. Luckily, we had satellite television by then and could beam Don out to the masses, so we had a way to keep Don out of the rinks, but still on television. I went to Harold Ballard, knowing the fondness the crusty Leafs' owner felt for the equally crusty television commentator — not to mention how much Pal Hal loved to annoy the other owners — and told him nobody wanted Don in their building.

Harold had no problem with Don being in Maple Leaf

Gardens — "He's welcome in my building anytime," he said — so we shot "Coach's Corner" there and simply broadcast it during intermissions of other games. In this respect, Ballard saved Don's career. Had he not allowed me to set Don up via satellite, Don could have been finished — we would have had nowhere else to go.

I moulded Don by not moulding him. The more syllables there were in a word, the better the chance Don was going to screw it up. And if he didn't like somebody, he'd go out of his way to flub the pronunciation of his name. That became evident with the influx of Europeans in the 1980s.

But we went through stuff with Don that hardly anybody knows about. For starters, the CBC brass forced him to go to language school. I wanted to keep Don on the air, but to do so, I knew I had to make compromises. The president of the CBC at that time, Pierre Juneau, made it clear that he didn't care what Don said, as long as he pronounced it properly.

Don went off to his first class, and the instructor had Don reciting mostly Shakespearean passages.

Cherry called me, furious.

"That fruit! I'm not going back to that fag."

As usual, I gave in to him.

"Fine. You went to one class. That's good enough. You passed."

The major thing I had to do was make sure Don was comfortable with what he was doing. Heaven knows he had no shortage of confidence, but television was an area he wasn't quite comfortable with yet. I knew in my heart he would get there. I treated him exactly the same way as I treated Howie. I said, "Don't you listen to anyone else ... be disciplined ... don't talk back to your producer ... do what you are told, but mainly, be yourself. And never be professional."

That's right, never.

When he is on a speaking engagement, Don tells people, "Mellanby told me not to become professional, and I always kept my word — I never did."

With Don, there was never really a comfort zone. Someone was always after him. In Vancouver, during the playoffs, one of our senior producers told him he had to speak proper English or he'd be fired.

Don called me and was frantic. I calmed him down.

"You just speak hockey. Everybody in a bar knows what you're talking about. Don't you worry about proper English."

He said, "I know I don't speak proper English good," then he laughed.

I only had Don for six years on *Hockey Night in Canada*, but I also started a weekly television show called *Don Cherry's Grapevine* that was syndicated across Canada, and that's when I really got to know him. I wanted to put Don in a situation on television where people could see that he knew more than just hockey — I knew he loved boxing and baseball and many other sports and he had a way of connecting with the athletes he admired — and this was the perfect vehicle for him.

We built a replica of a bar in a studio in Hamilton, Ontario, and for the first show we had two days of rehearsal so Don would be comfortable on the set. I went backstage prior to the first show and Don was shaking like a leaf. He was drop-dead nervous. I had never seen him like this. Normally, Don is beyond cool and way past controlled. In my position as executive producer, I decided I wanted to always be close to Don on the floor, not stuck away in some booth. I'm glad I made that decision.

How could I help this blossoming television star? Simple. I held his hand to give him comfort and support. And right away, he stopped shaking and walked onto the set.

We used to tape two shows at a time at the beginning, and eventually we'd do three at a time. I used to walk up the street to get people to come in and sit in the audience for the taping. We didn't air the shows in order; we'd run Muhammad Ali or Duke Snider in between hockey shows. But the guests on the first two shows we produced were Bobby Orr and Wayne Gretzky. You couldn't pick two better players: the best player Don ever coached, by now well into his premature retirement from numerous knee injuries, and the best player who ever played the game, in the infancy of his career.

Ultimately, Don grew into the superstar of Canadian television. As good a coach as he was, it was television that turned him into a household name. He opened a chain of restaurants bearing his name; became a spokesman for numerous products, including tires, life insurance and cold medication; and has a daily radio feature with Brian Williams that plays all across Canada.

And as much as the CBC tried to tame him, it never could. Don pretty much did what Don wanted to do.

Don loved to pay homage to Canadian soldiers, particularly those who gave their lives so others could enjoy freedom. On March 22, 2003, Don went off about how Canadians weren't supporting the United States in its military operation in Iraq. Dressed in a red, white and blue tie, Don ripped the Canadian government for its lack of support for our neighbours to the south.

It was clearly a contentious issue, and Don made it clear where he stood. Many were upset that he used his position as a television sports announcer to deliver political diatribes. With Don, there are no grey areas and no compromise.

I loved his defiance. I'd say I disagree with about 90 percent of what Don says on the air. Like Howie Meeker, I love skill. One of the things I would do is ban fighting in hockey — to me, it's a waste of time — and I know Don would never agree to that.

Don hates it when referees call marginal penalties. Always has. He thinks the players should decide the outcome of a game. In Don's perfect world, there would be no referees and the winner would be the survivor in a battle of the fittest. Maybe it's because he was a plugger and identifies with players who lack skill, but make up for it in courage.

Don has always had a chip on his shoulder. He was a career minor-leaguer who never got his chance. He feels that with expansion, when the NHL doubled in size from six teams to twelve, he would have made it, and I am certain he would have.

He got a huge chip on his shoulder about the Europeans in 1981 when he was hired to coach Canada at the World Championship and he felt that Canada got screwed by the European officials. Canada iced its strongest team since returning to international competition in 1977, with such players as Wayne Gretzky, Bobby Clarke and Darryl Sittler, but call after call went against Canada and Don was convinced the European refs were conspiring to make sure Canada didn't win a medal. A bad call went against Canada, robbing Don and his team of a trip to the podium, and I don't think he has ever forgotten it.

Say what you want about Don, but the one thing I know is that if he's your friend, he is your friend for life. If you have to walk through a back alley and fight five guys to make it through, he's the guy you want walking beside you. He is the most loyal man I have ever met.

Don loves saunas, and has one in his house. At home, he dresses like a ragbag in an old sweatsuit — the antithesis of who he is in public. He plays the bagpipes, and has one of the largest collections of Wedgwood china plates I have ever seen — they're displayed all around his den. He says the only people ever allowed into his home to watch a hockey game with him are his son Tim, Bobby Orr and Ralph Mellanby.

Don loves history, especially British military history, and his hero is Lord Nelson. He used to get up in front of the Bruins and quote Nelson. One day, a player — I am certain it was Cherry's little tough guy, Stan Jonathan — asked, "What wing does this guy Nelson play?"

He is a great family man and a Christian. Above all, he loves Canada. He spent a lot of his career in the United States, but he loves Canada. He's a little touchy on Quebec, but...

It is an amazing thing to me that we have two official languages in Canada, and Don Cherry became Canada's greatest television star even though he doesn't speak either one of them.

My only regret is that, when he finished in the top ten among the greatest Canadians, he wasn't number one.

Chapter 9

THE (OTHER) BOYS OF SATURDAY NIGHT

The idea to write this book originated with my children: Scott, who at the time of this writing has just retired from a lengthy NHL career, and Laura, who is a television executive in her own right. They said they loved hearing my stories and felt that they would make a great book, especially for my grandchildren.

One of the best parts of this process has been the chance to share my thoughts and memories about so many of the wonderful people I've worked with. My only regret is that there wasn't enough room in just one book. I haven't even mentioned voices like Mike Anscombe, Chris Cuthbert, Bill Good, Steve Armitage, Scott Oake, Jim Van Horne, John Wells, Gilles Tremblay and René Lecavalier, my favourite announcer from the French broadcast. Or Red Storey, the longtime NHL referee who appeared frequently on our show, especially at Christmastime, when he always played Santa Claus. Or the outspoken Dick Beddoes, who made our "Hot Stove Lounge" segments and the post-game show, "Overtime," so memorable.

I also look forward to one day writing more about my best pal, Glen Sather, as well as such star players as Rod Gilbert, Marcel Dionne, Milt Schmidt, Ken Dryden, Red Kelly, Stan Mikita and Paul Henderson, plus Hall of Fame general managers like Punch Imlach and Sam Pollock. Of course, I knew coaches like Al Arbour, Fred Shero and Roger Neilson — oh, the stories I could tell about them!

In one of his columns, Jim Coleman wrote that, in the 1970s and

'80s, there was in one place the greatest array of talent — in front of *and* behind the camera — in the history of Canadian television. He was writing, of course, about *Hockey Night in Canada.*

It's a source of great pride for me that the producers and directors I hired for *Hockey Night* now run the sports television industry in Canada. John Shannon is the vice-president of broadcasting for the NHL. Doug Beeforth, who also worked for me at the Olympics, is the president of Rogers Sportsnet, while Rick Briggs-Jude is his executive producer. Doug Sellars is now executive producer of Fox Sports in the United States. Rick Brace, our commercial producer at CBC, is now president of the CTV Network and TSN. François Carignan is now executive producer of Radio-Canada's Olympic team.

Ron Harrison and Jacques Primeau, our top directors, have been honoured several times and are revered, along with the late George Retzlaff, as the finest directors in Canada's television sports history. Thank you all for the memories!

To close out this part of the book, I'd like to fit in some short takes about just a few more of those talented people.

JACK DENNETT THE PATRIARCH OF *HNIC*

I used to listen to Jack Dennett when I was a little boy. When I started at *Hockey Night in Canada,* it was very obvious that everybody revered Jack Dennett because he was *the* newscaster in Canada. He had larger ratings in the Toronto area than all the others across the country put together. He was the voice of CFRB radio news, and his shows were syndicated in a day and age before syndication was popular.

Dennett, Foster Hewitt and Danny Gallivan were our link to the past on *Hockey Night.* Foster was there from the beginning, of course, while Jack had been part of the "Hot Stove League" since the show was in its infancy. The amazing thing was that the "Hot Stove League" was actually scripted. Listeners had the impression that it was a free-for-all of hockey chit-chat, but they actually stuck to a script — because of security concerns related to the war. *Hockey Night in Canada* was the first radio show to have recordings sent overseas to the troops, and the government didn't want anybody slipping any information into the dialogue. It sounds funny today, but back then it was a major concern.

The "Hot Stove League" was a tradition; everybody listened to it on the radio. The host was CFRB sportscaster Wes McKnight, and the panel included Bobby Hewitson, Elmer Ferguson and Court Benson. All of them became household names. Then, when games started to be televised, the "Hot Stove League" aired during the intermissions. It didn't work well, but it was part of the tradition. At least the show wasn't scripted then.

Jack had been one of our great war correspondents, and all the talent on *Hockey Night in Canada* really looked up to him. He was a great mentor to our young host, Dave Hodge, who didn't always listen to me, but listened to Jack and valued his experience.

I used Jack in various ways. He did all the voice-overs on our films and segment bridges. He also did our obituaries. In fact, I'd call him and say, "We need you right away, Jack, for a voicer."

And he'd reply, "Who died?"

The great thing about Dennett was that he'd always show up on Saturday night in his blue *Hockey Night in Canada* outfit, ready to go. He would already have pre-recorded his stuff for the show in the morning or afternoon, and chances were that he wouldn't be used again in the broadcast. But, he'd say, "Just in case you need me, I'm here." What a team player.

I'd use Jack in panel discussions, especially on topics with historical significance or a news angle. Later in Jack's career, after the Vancouver Canucks started, I needed a *Hockey Night in Canada* personality for those games. Jack and I would fly out to Vancouver — always first class — and he really enjoyed being part of those broadcasts, as the third man up in the booth with Jim Robson and Bill Good Jr. He did a hell of a job as an analyst; he also really cemented the team because he was identified with *Hockey Night in Canada*, while the other guys had never been associated with our show. He often reminded me that — while he only did eight or ten appearances a year — he belonged on the show because his father had built a great fountain in Stanley Park. He was an important element in our west coast broadcasts, as he brought a great sense of history and celebrity to them.

I always enjoyed those trips out west because he would tell great stories on the trip. He was a great pal of Winston Churchill and Edward R. Murrow, and would tell stories about Churchill and Eisenhower and others.

Jack Dennett was our historian and the patriarch of the show. He died in 1975, and his absence from *Hockey Night in Canada* left a little hole in our hearts.

TED REYNOLDS A BROADCASTING LEGEND

When the NHL granted a franchise to Vancouver, I went out west to set things up, and I ran into Ted Reynolds at the CBC there. He said, "Well, I guess you're going to bring in all the guys from Toronto to do our show."

"No, I'm not," I replied. "I want to use local guys."

That surprised him. Ted was a very parochial, pro-B.C. kind of guy. He was also a big star on the west coast. There was no other choice for the hosting job, though I didn't tell him so at the time.

I asked him who the best guys were, and he said, "Jim Robson is the best play-by-play man, but you'll never get him off radio." He then proceeded to help me influence Robson's station to release him on Saturday nights, which he could do, because he was the best-connected broadcaster in western Canada. He helped me open doors in order to get the job done. Nobody in Vancouver said no to Reynolds. Hiring Ted as our host gave us immediate credibility out west.

Even though he was already established as a star — he had called all kinds of great events, from the Olympics to the historic Bannister–Landry match race at the 1954 Empire Games in

Vancouver — he told me that working on *Hockey Night in Canada* was a dream come true. I'm sure that, as the years went along, Ted never lost his dislike for the Eastern brass. But for us, he was easy to direct and a real pro. In fact, he made our Vancouver shows. I owe him and was very happy when he received Sports Canada's highest honour — a Lifetime Achievement Award.

JIM ROBSON THE PACIFIC STAR

As the NHL expanded, I thought it was very important that different regions throughout the country be represented on Hockey Night in Canada. When Vancouver joined the NHL in 1970, many assumed I would just bring Bill Hewitt and Brian McFarlane into Vancouver to do the Canucks' games. But I wanted a local crew with only one *Hockey Night in Canada* guy.

When I started my research into who might be available, Ted Hough told me to go after Jim Robson. I didn't know his work, but it turned out he'd been calling games for the old Canucks of the Western Hockey League, as well as B.C. Lions football and Vancouver Mounties Triple-A baseball. I got his tapes from both television and radio and immediately felt that he'd be perfect for the job of calling the Canucks' play-by-play. He didn't sound like Bob Cole or Danny Gallivan or Foster Hewitt; he had his own unique way of calling games, with a staccato style that made him sound almost like an American broadcaster.

When I first met with him at the Hotel Vancouver, one of the first things he asked was, "Who is going to replace me on radio on Saturday nights?" You'd expect someone to be thrilled at the prospect of joining the *Hockey Night* crew, of doing the same job as legends like Hewitt and Gallivan. Instead, he was more worried about who was going to do the Canucks on radio!

I told him, "That's your problem."

He didn't ask about the money or working conditions. He was very unemotional about the whole thing — very cool and professional.

Jim and I still hadn't worked out a deal by the time the NHL Canucks made their *Hockey Night in Canada* debut, so I had to fly Gallivan in to call the action. The Canucks didn't have another game with us for a month, and by the time it rolled around, Jim and I finally had made a deal.

Jim always felt that he wasn't as highly regarded as the other play-by-play men. It took me a while to get him to understand that we felt he was a very valuable member of our team. To prove it, I gave him an NHL All-Star Game, and then assigned him to the Stanley Cup finals in 1980, between the Philadelphia Flyers and the New York Islanders. Whenever the finals involved two U.S. teams, all the play-by-play voices wanted the job. Jim was amazed that I chose him, but I felt he had earned it. And he definitely did not let me down!

Jim wasn't good on camera, but he learned very quickly and well. Right from the beginning he was the ultimate professional. He was never a problem for me. He'd show up, do a beautiful job and then leave. And the more he worked on a national stage, the better he was. I also liked his character.

That said, you never felt like you were close to him. He could be distant. He was a clean-living guy, and didn't smoke, drink or go out with the guys because he really never grew close to any of the guys on the crew.

My regret with Jim was that I didn't use him enough. He was under contract to call Canucks games on the radio, and under that deal was only available to us on Saturday nights and during the playoffs. Otherwise, I would have used him in Calgary, Winnipeg and Edmonton. Anyway, it meant he didn't appear much on *Hockey Night in Canada* until the Canucks were out of the playoffs — which, fortunately for us, was quite often in those days. Today, Robson's protégé, Jim Hughson, is used a lot on the national telecasts.

Jim Robson retired in 1999, and I think it was way too early. He was Mr. Vancouver and should have stayed on the air longer. He was still at the top of his game.

The Vancouver crew, with Ted Reynolds as host, Babe Pratt as analyst and Bill Good Jr. as a specialty act, was excellent right from the start. Jim Robson was the star attraction, though, and that is why today he is in the Hockey Hall of Fame.

DON WITTMAN HOCKEY NIGHT'S WESTERN VOICE

> "The ultimate professional." — John Hudson, former head of CBC Sports and TV Labatt, about Don Wittman

In 1979, the National Hockey League added Edmonton and Winnipeg (and Quebec, which was not part of the *Hockey Night in Canada* package) when the World Hockey Association disbanded. Then, a year later, came Calgary, when the Atlanta Flames moved north. Once again, I was faced with the challenge of finding new play-by-play talent for the additional telecasts.

Expansion didn't only affect the product on the ice, where teams were scrambling to find enough quality players. It also left me facing the possibility that my crews would be stretched thinner by the extra work. By this time, I had been working with the CBC on the Toronto Blue Jays baseball broadcasts, and I decided it was time to hire someone from the CBC to work on *Hockey Night.* It was time to get over the notion that we always had to hire freelancers.

I knew of Don Wittman's work and knew many people who held him in the highest regard. Among other events, he had covered curling, football and the Olympics for the CBC going back to the early 1960s. Don was a westerner, and while he was an extremely confident broadcaster, the western guys were always a little different. What I mean is, they always seemed to feel like second-class citizens in Canada. They had a bit of a chip on their shoulder, especially where Toronto was concerned. The attitude seemed to be "Poor us. Everything is run out of Toronto — including *Hockey Night in Canada.*" The way I finally overcame that was by opening a western office in Calgary around 1980. We ran all the western telecasts out of that office, and I think it showed everyone our commitment to the western Canadian teams in the league. John Shannon ran things for us, and he had his own people there. It was a good political move for us.

The thing about Wittman was that, no matter who sat next to him in the booth, it was as if they had worked together forever. Don has the ability to bring out the best in his analyst and really use him well. I used that to my advantage. If I was having trouble with Gary Dornhoefer or Mickey Redmond, I'd put them with Wittman. Don is so good that you could give him a tiddlywinks match to announce and he'd call a great game. He doesn't have any "Don Wittmanisms"; he just calls a beautiful game, whether it's hockey, football or curling.

The years I worked with Don were a dream — I only wish there had been more of them. He became, along with Robson, our western voices. Recently, Don was given the sportscaster of the year award by Sports Media Canada. He is still "on" and still great — a Canadian treasure.

TED DARLING ONE OF THE BEST, AND ONE OF THE FUNNIEST

> "Today, I am a star!" — a smirking Ted Darling to the crew upon joining *Hockey Night in Canada*

When Ted Darling heard that an opening was coming up on *Hockey Night*, he called me from Ottawa and asked, "What are you going to do in Montreal?"

I confirmed that I was looking for somebody. "Are you interested?" I asked.

"This is a job I know I can do," he said. "I'll be your number one star. Just give me a chance."

The position he got was Dan Kelly's job as host in Montreal after

Dan left us to work in St. Louis.

To be honest, I don't think Ted gave the best audition, but there was something about him that sold me. He was brimming with confidence. He was from the Ottawa Valley, and I didn't want to bring in a Toronto guy for Sam Pollock's approval.

I went to Ottawa and spent three days with him, going over my philosophy and guidelines. If Ted had one weakness at the start, it was that he didn't prepare himself very well. After his first couple of appearances, I told him, "You know, you won't be the star you think you can be if you don't start preparing more."

I told him I wanted more input from him. "Who do you want to interview? Let me know — we'll make it happen. Get involved."

Dave Hodge was the best at that, picking his own interviews and presenting ideas.

The first year rolled along nicely, and on the day of our first playoff game, we were in a Boston hotel having a meeting, and there was no sign of Ted — our host wasn't at the meeting. Needless to say, I wasn't thrilled.

Suddenly, the phone rang.

It was Ted. "Hey, look out the window," he said. "There's a naked man."

We looked out the window, and there he was ... naked and laughing and waving at us!

That was Ted in a nutshell: one of the funniest men I ever met in our business. His sense of humour was unbelievable, and he had a love of the absurd. He loved people and he loved a good joke.

On another occasion, he was telling us about being recognized for the first time while taking the train from Ottawa to Montreal.

"There I was in the coach car with my blue *Hockey Night in Canada* jacket on, and this drunk walks up to me and says, 'You're the guy from *Hockey Night in Canada*, aren't you?'

"I said, 'Yes.'

"He says, 'You're the guy who comes on and says, "Welcome to the Forum and *Hockey Night in Canada*."'"

"Again I say, 'Yes. I'm Ted Darling.'

"And *I* always say, 'Who gives a shit?'"

Of course, he made up the whole story, but he had everybody laughing. That was Ted. Of course, there's at least one grain of truth in that story: Ted always hoped to be recognized when he went out in public.

Dick and Danny were the greatest broadcasting team ever, but they weren't exactly social animals. They never went out with the guys. Danny would go to his room, while Dick might go to a movie — usually with me.

Ted, on the other hand, was just plain fun. And he loved the profession. He never looked at his job with *HNiC* as a stepping stone; he felt like he was going to be there forever.

Ted worked for *Hockey Night* for two years and then left us to call play-by-play for the Buffalo Sabres. He told me that they were offering him big money, and I said we couldn't match it.

I said, "Ted, you'd be crazy not to take that job." I told him Buffalo would be a solid franchise, and with *Hockey Night* he might think he was number one, but in reality he would be a little lower in the pecking order. I told him he would be a big star in Buffalo, and that is exactly what happened. He never would have had the chance to call the Stanley Cup finals with us, but he did it with the Sabres in 1975.

I said I hated to lose him, but he had to take the job. The one piece of advice I gave him was to just be himself and not try to be Danny Gallivan.

The end was sad for Ted. I got a call from Paul Whalen, the head of broadcasting for the Sabres, who was gravely concerned. He told me Ted was making horrible mistakes during broadcasts. Ted used to love his rum and Cokes — as did old "Ralphie" — but Ted never drank on the job.

Paul said, "Ralph, I think the alcohol is eating away at his brain. I have to replace him."

I didn't think it was the alcohol — he was in his mid-fifties, too young for it to be affecting him that way. Without investigating the real problem, they took him off the air and replaced him with Rick Jeanneret in the middle of the season. That's the NHL for you.

Soon afterward, I talked to his wife, Sheila, who told me he was in the early stages of Alzheimer's disease. I also spoke with Ted, and while he wasn't himself, he wasn't that bad.

A year later, on the day he was inducted into the Hall of Fame, he wandered away from the hotel in Toronto and was lost. Everybody was worried and out looking for him, and they found him a couple of miles away, wandering around the Eaton Centre. It was very sad on a day when he was being enshrined, because I'm not even sure he knew the Hockey Hall of Fame was honouring him.

Ted loved life, loved his family and was a good husband. He didn't have a long life, but during his career I never saw Ted Darling without a smile on his face — even on the golf course or tennis court.

Today, his son, Joel, has my old job at *Hockey Night in Canada* and is doing a fine job as executive producer. Ted's brother, Hal Kelly, was a star on CBC in the early days and did baseball for the network.

It's strange to look back now at the Three Broadcast Musketeers of Ottawa, all best friends: Dan Kelly, Pat Marsden and Ted Darling. I will never forget my visit to Ottawa when Ted and Dan introduced me to Pat. Pat's first words to me were, "Your intermissions are dull! You need controversy." (He was right, and I was about to add the great Howie Meeker for that very reason.)

I asked Pat, "Who would you suggest?"

Marsden said, "Me — I'm the only choice."

Today, Pat is in the Football Hall of Fame and the Sports Media Canada Hall of Fame, while Ted and Dan are in the broadcast section of the Hockey Hall of Fame. Now they are all gone — having died way too soon. I miss them terribly, but I was lucky to have known them.

Here's to you, Ted, and I do give a shit. I am proud to have called the voice of the Buffalo Sabres my friend. When we meet again, have the rum and Coke ready.

JOHN DAVIDSON THE FIRST GOALIE ANALYST

John Shannon, one of our great producers, deserves the credit for John Davidson being hired on *Hockey Night in Canada*. Shannon knew he was a very good goaltender with the St. Louis Blues and New York Rangers, and felt John had both the knowledge and temperament to be a television star.

I didn't really agree, but respected Shannon's intuition. He really pushed to get Davidson hired. From my perspective, Davidson was a good hire politically, because he was from the west and had just retired from the game. I also found him to be a gregarious character, full of life, with a great sense of humour. I didn't think he'd be the greatest hockey analyst in television history, but that is exactly what he became.

Davidson was fresh off a very solid ten-year NHL career split between the St. Louis Blues and the New York Rangers, and had been the first goalie to move directly into the big leagues from junior without first spending time in the minor leagues. While he wasn't a spectacular stopper, he was a heart and soul player who completed his career with a 123–124–39 record — not bad, actually, when you consider that he played on some mediocre teams. His shining moment came in 1978–79, when he led the Rangers to the Stanley Cup finals, only to lose in five games to the Montreal Canadiens.

I'll never forget Davidson's television debut, at Maple Leaf Gardens in Toronto. We put him in the booth as the third man with Bill Hewitt and Brian McFarlane. He'd had some training, but we wanted to break him in slowly, and those two were pros who would teach him the ropes.

John, like many athletes, perspires a lot. At first, we didn't realize exactly how much. We wanted to get him on camera as soon as possible, to establish his presence. We had him slated to go on between the first and second periods. But during the first period, I got a call saying, "Immediate help is needed for the intermission. We need towels and the makeup girl."

John was soaking wet! Thank God we had pre-taped the opening in the gondola!

During the second period, another call: "We don't think he's going to be able to go on air! His jacket is all sweaty and his shirt is drenched."

I took off my own shirt and jacket and sent them upstairs. Fortunately for me, we had a sweatshirt kicking around the studio that I could wear. Here was the executive producer, working in a Leafs shirt. So much for not being a homer.

John was so nervous. For every game he ever did for us, I told the crew to make sure there were ten towels upstairs for him and that the makeup girl was always ready. I also ordered a backup shirt and jacket for him.

On the air, however, he was no problem. He got it right away. I can't remember anybody being so good so quickly. It was as though broadcasting was a profession that was made for him. The quality that John had, which I liked a lot, was that he had just come off the ice, so his take on the game was still very fresh.

I always had a feeling that goaltenders would make the best analysts, because they saw the whole rink when they played. John was the first that we hired, and he paved the way for a flood of others: Glenn Healy, Darren Pang, John Garrett, Kelly Hrudey, Kay Whitmore, Chico Resch, Bobby Taylor, Daryl Reaugh ... the list goes on and on. And all of those guys owe John a vote of thanks.

Hockey Night in Canada couldn't afford to keep him; he eventually moved to the United States to do network and local television. However, he continued to make appearances on the between-periods "Satellite Hot Stove" sessions, right up until 2006, when he was named president of the St. Louis Blues. My guess is he'll do just fine. No sweat!

HARRY NEALE A SMART GM IN THE BOOTH

For my money, coaches rank right up there with goaltenders as analysts. Case in point: Harry Neale. Neale had coached in the WHA with the Minnesota Fighting Saints and New England Whalers, as well as with the Vancouver Canucks and Detroit Red Wings in the NHL. I had my eye on him for a long time; to me, getting him on the show was a no-brainer. From the very beginning, he was a wonderful analyst, not to mention a great storyteller. The thing that really stood out for me was his sense of humour.

When Harry joined the show in 1985–86, he had just been let go by the Red Wings. He could relate to the present, because he hadn't been out of the game for ten years. Hell, he wasn't out of the game for ten minutes! I didn't think he'd last long on *HNiC* because I was convinced he'd soon return to the NHL as general manager or president of a team.

We could use Harry with anybody, but there can be no doubt that he has more chemistry with Bob Cole than with others. They were — and still are — a great team.

The thing that Harry brought to his show, and still does, is his unusual style and humour. I'll never forget his classic quip from the days when he was coaching the Canucks and they were having a heck of a time trying to win games.

"We can't win at home and we can't win on the road," he said. "My failing as coach is in not being able to find someplace else for us to play."

The year my son, Scott, was being drafted, we were having the NHL meetings in Montreal and I had to meet a very beautiful woman from McLaren Advertising for a business meeting. I offered to buy her dinner. Harry, who was with Vancouver at the time, walked into the restaurant with one of his chief scouts and pointed to me and said, "You see Mellanby over there? That's the reason I'm not drafting his kid. No character."

He was such a great joker — or was he serious?

I am happy that Harry has enjoyed such a great career, but I'm also a little disappointed for him because I felt he was a great hockey man. I think he would have done an excellent job for any team and was surprised when he didn't get back into the game, especially with expansion.

He's been behind a microphone for a long time, but in my opinion he's still at the top of his game. He's not afraid to express his opinion, but he does it in such away that he doesn't make enemies. Today, as a fan sitting at home, I can say that Harry is still my favourite analyst and, in my humble experience, the best. As I told him at his seventieth birthday party, "Harry, do the fans a favour — don't ever retire."

RON MACLEAN THE GREAT SURPRISE

Ron was in our "farm system" when I left *Hockey Night in Canada*. (We owned all the Canadian teams' local rights in those days, and we used to call the local NHL broadcasts our farm system.) MacLean came from Red Deer, Alberta, and we hired him to be the host in Calgary and Edmonton. He was another Shannon guy, and John backed him. I liked him as a person, but didn't really care for his performance.

I would look at his tapes and say, "Geez, I don't think MacLean will ever make it. He's too corny." To me, he came across as a bit of a hayseed, not as a big-time network announcer.

"Don't worry," Shannon said. "I'll work with him."

On another occasion, Shannon said, "Ralph, someday this guy will not only make the big *Hockey Night in Canada* team, but he will be the best host we ever had."

"Never!" I said.

Wrong again, Ralph.

He didn't have the right look to me. He was no Dave Hodge, I'll tell you that. If I had stayed with the show, Ron would never have replaced Hodge. But the new executive producer, Ron Harrison, loved his work. MacLean was probably lucky I left, and so was *Hockey Night in Canada*, because I was wrong about him.

By the time Ron replaced Hodge (after the pencil-throwing incident), he was greatly improved. It was obvious that he really worked at his style, though he still had his detractors. Ron turned out great, the best in the business, to the credit of the people who followed me. I love to watch him today and enjoy his outspoken approach.

He hosts the Olympics and all sorts of major CBC events, something none of our other hosts ever accomplished. He and Don Cherry have become *the* team — the look and the brand of the current *Hockey Night in Canada* presentations.

Sorry, Ron, I was out of line.

MICKEY REDMOND AND GARY DORNHOEFER
OFF THE ICE, INTO THE BOOTH

My fondness for ex-goalies as analysts doesn't mean I would rule out skaters as having what it took to be great analysts. In fact, two of my very best were forwards: Gary Dornhoefer, an industrious winger with the Philadelphia Flyers, and Mickey Redmond, a sharp-shooting two-time fifty-goal scorer with the Detroit Red Wings.

Dornhoefer didn't really want to work on television after he retired; I had to pursue him. He had retired after playing fourteen years in the NHL with the Boston Bruins and Philadelphia Flyers. I was a great admirer of Gary's, because he wasn't flashy but was tough and honest. I never saw a hockey player work harder with limited skill than he did — and what a heart! He suffered numerous injuries, but still he played on. Before hiring Gary, I checked with my old pal, Bobby Clarke, who told me how much his teammates had appreciated Gary. Because of the Flyers' success — they won Stanley Cups in 1974 and '75 — Gary was a well-known player, and he retired moderately early (in 1978, at thirty-five) because of all the injuries.

I called him to see if he'd be interested in working with *Hockey Night in Canada* and invited him to one of our training sessions. He was very reticent and said he'd have to think about it. I think the notion of having to commute from Philadelphia really didn't sit too well with him, although eventually he moved back to Kitchener, Ontario, so travel was no longer an issue.

What he had been as a player, he was as a broadcaster. He was hard-working and always prepared — in fact, he was over-prepared. I started him as the third man in the booth, as I had done with so many others, and he quickly became our key analyst. He and Redmond, who also enjoyed some fine seasons playing with Montreal and Detroit, were our first analysts to come directly from the game. To me, this recent experience was important, because most of the players they had played against were still active. They had first-hand knowledge of those players and had great knowledge of the teams.

If I had to use only one word to describe Gary, it would be "dependable." It didn't matter who he worked with, he fit in and always did a solid job for us. NHL general managers must have shared my opinion, because many of them told me he was a good hire and that he brought a lot of new information to the show. Though he scored 20 goals five times, Gary was never a great scorer, so he concentrated on the defensive side of the game. He was a class act and represented our show very well at all sorts of occasions. Viewers really seemed to take to him; he acquired a huge following. In 1980, after the Stanley Cup finals on Long Island, I put Gary on skates to interview players — a first for the show. He got a real kick out of doing that.

* * *

Mickey Redmond had a great mind. He was different from Gary in that he loved offence and looked at the game from that point of view. He also talked me into using the isolation camera on the great offensive stars.

After he was forced to retire from the game in 1976 because of back problems, Mickey appeared on a television show I produced called *The Original Six*, which was a series of games between retired NHLers representing the "Original Six" teams. Mickey came up to me during a taping and said he'd really like to get into broadcasting.

I knew Mickey as a player and liked him. He was a bit of a free spirit, and he brought that personality to the broadcast arena, which made for outstanding chemistry when I combined him with Bob Cole. People think about broadcast teams like Gallivan and Irvin and don't realize that they weren't close friends away from the rink. They just worked together, and maybe played golf together once a year. They weren't close. Cole and Redmond, though, loved to hang out together. On the road, they would arrange for adjoining hotel rooms, and they would love to share a drink — as well as their love of the sport — after games.

What Mickey brought, also, was imagination and humour. He loved to laugh and he made the broadcasts fun, especially for Bob. Redmond was also a great-looking guy, which helped him become a media star.

I thought both Gary and Mickey were excellent on *Hockey Night in Canada*, yet when I left, neither had their contract renewed. That disappointed me greatly. The funny thing is that both went on to have long careers as respected broadcasters — Mickey is still on the air, working Detroit Red Wings games, while Gary left the Philadelphia Flyers booth in 2006. I am proud of both of them. Together they added a new element to *Hockey Night in Canada*, starting a trend by coming directly from the ice to the broadcast booth.

BOB GOLDHAM MR. CONSISTENCY

In the 1960s, Bob Goldham was the first guy we tried in a permanent in-studio role, and he made it work, first with Ward Cornell and later with Dave Hodge. He preceded both Howie Meeker and Don Cherry and set a very high standard as a between-periods analyst. In fact, he invented the role.

We never auditioned Bob — we just put him on the air, and he was great from the get-go. Bob Gordon, our senior producer, interviewed him and just had a feeling he would be solid on television. He had character and an innately likeable manner that really came through and contributed directly to his great popularity. He wasn't controversial, but he'd tell it the way he saw it — plainly, and never with an edge.

I had watched him play defence with the great Red Wing teams of the '50s when I was a boy in Essex, and before that he'd played for the Leafs, appearing on four Stanley Cup teams in his career. (By the way, I'm amazed that he's not in the Hockey Hall of Fame, because he was the best shot-blocker in the history of the game.)

"Goldie," as we called him, really embraced *Hockey Night in Canada*. We had a basketball team we called the Hockey Knights, and he would play with us. He had a great two-handed set shot. Then he played on our softball team, too. He was part of our culture and loved his role on the show.

I remember telling him about the telestrator, and he wanted no part of it.

"It's not for me," he'd say. "I like doing things the way I always have done them. Give it to Meeker." That, by the way, really made Howie's career.

After many years, Bob was phased out of the show. I was gone by then, and the others who were loyal to Bob were gone, too. New people were in charge and they wanted their people on the show. But he'll always be a favourite of mine. You wouldn't find a more decent guy than Bob Goldham.

GEORGE GROSS WORLD HOCKEY REPORTER

In the wake of the 1972 Summit Series, North Americans — and Canadians in particular — really had their eyes opened. We'd figured we had cornered the market on hockey and were the only ones who knew how to play the game properly. The Russians showed us otherwise, especially with their unique new systems. As a result, Canadian audiences suddenly had a thirst for international hockey. It was an opportunity for us, as well as a challenge.

I knew George Gross, a columnist with the *Toronto Telegram* and then the *Toronto Sun*, very well. He was a great friend of Leafs coach Punch Imlach, and I had seen him on many panels and liked his work. Also, he was my neighbour; I used to spend every New Year's Eve at George's house, rubbing elbows with the cream of Toronto's sports royalty — folks like Steve Stavro and Red Kelly.

One New Year's Eve in the late '70s, I told George that what I'd like to do over the summer was go to Europe and film features about players and the game in general over there. "The World Hockey Report" was born. It ran as a monthly intermission feature on *Hockey Night in Canada*, and the idea was to give Canadians a look at what was going on in hockey outside North America. At the time, George and I thought the NHL would be a global league one day. I never dreamed it would end up in places like Nashville and Florida; I figured the next wave of expansion teams would be in Moscow and Prague.

George was born in 1923 in Bratislava, Czechoslovakia, and he knew everyone who was anyone in international hockey. At speaking engagements, I joke that when the first astronaut lands on Mars, the Martians will ask, "Where are you from?"

"I'm from the planet Earth."

"Oh," they'll reply. "Do you know George Gross?"

George really taught me about international hockey and introduced me to all the top people in the sport. He picked the subjects we would cover, and he had a long list of people he felt we needed to bring to the audience's attention. He did the research and appeared in the segments. His aristocratic appearance and Slovak accent only reinforced to viewers that he knew his way around the hockey world — this wasn't just another Canadian reporter yakking about the international game.

We went to see Tommy "Shotgun" Simpson, who played in Holland after his time in the World Hockey Association, and Garry Monahan, who played 748 games in the NHL and closed out his career in Japan. And, of course, we also visited the hockey hotbeds in Russia, Czechoslovakia, Sweden, Finland and so on. Among others, it gave Canadians their first look at the Stastny brothers.

George has been inducted into numerous Halls of Fame. He was presented with the Hockey Hall of Fame's Elmer Ferguson Memorial Award in 1985; received the Olympic Order in 1994; was inducted into the Order of Ontario in 2003 and Canada's Sports Hall of Fame in 2005; and was named to the Canadian Soccer Hall of Fame as a builder in 2006.

Whenever we had an international story, I'd throw together a panel to talk about it and would always include George on it. He was our resident authority.

Gross was worldly and loved to travel and have a good time. One night, while we were filming in Austria, it was my wife Janet's birthday, so George took us out to his favourite restaurant. A four-piece band came over to our table to entertain us, playing all of Janet's favourite songs. It was really a wonderful night.

Afterwards, with George having picked up the cheque for the meal — he used to joke that he was a Slovak who like to pick up the Czech — I decided to tip the entertainers because they had been so nice to us. So I gave them $100, which was quite a lot of money back in those days. The next thing I knew, they were following us down the street back to our hotel, still serenading Janet. They walked three blocks with us.

The next morning I woke up and joined George for breakfast. I told him about the musicians following us back to our hotel.

"No wonder," he said. "I tipped them $100."

"What?" I exclaimed. "*I* tipped them $100!"

"Geez," he said. "They should have followed us back to Canada for that kind of money."

RED FISHER THE FISHER REPORT

Being from a journalistic family, I wanted there to be someone on *Hockey Night in Canada* who would break stories. And Red Fisher was the most famous English-speaking hockey reporter in Montreal, so we put him under contract to do a feature called "The Fisher Report" roughly every three weeks. We teamed Red with Dick Irvin, and he talked about whatever he wanted.

Red was with us twenty years, but there was a pause in the middle when we had to fire him because David Molson, who owned the Montreal Canadiens, disagreed with something he said and put pressure on my boss to let him go. That's the way it was in those days — though I'm certain owners and sponsors still try to pressure the networks. What happened was that Red had received a confidential report from the NHL and leaked a story through his column in the Montreal *Gazette*. The only way Molson could retaliate was to have him fired from *HNiC*.

I didn't fire Red, but I was the one who had to call him. I said, "Sorry, Red, but I can't use you anymore. You're under an embargo." But I promised him I'd get him back on the air eventually.

Red hung up the phone rather gruffly, but that was Red. He's a tough guy in a lot of ways.

Two years later, I kept my promise and got Red back. The Canadiens' ownership had changed, and Irving Grundman took over the team. My first request was to be allowed to revive "The Fisher Report." Grundman wasn't general manager yet, but he said, "Fine. No problem," and Red came back to the show.

It always pissed me off — and I told Red so — that in his book *Hockey, Heroes, and Me* he wrote about being fired but didn't mention me getting him back on *Hockey Night* — and he was on for many years after the incident.

Red was very comfortable on camera, soft-spoken and humorous, easy and natural. I couldn't find anybody in Toronto, Edmonton or Vancouver to match him. Normally, the segments aired live, but there were times when I would tape them because his stories could be a little bit charged and I didn't want Red or the show to land in trouble. Sometimes, the stories Red "broke" were only rumours, but he wasn't afraid to cover a controversial story on television and then follow up on it in his newspaper column.

It's not that Red improved our ratings, but he was the kind of guy our audience would listen to and believe. And he and Dick played well off one another.

Red was phased out after I left, but of all the segments I produced for *Hockey Night in Canada* — from "Pro Tips" to "The World Hockey Report" to "Showdown" — my favourite was "The Fisher Report."

BABE PRATT MR. ENTERTAINMENT

When the Vancouver Canucks joined the NHL in 1970, I had to put together a crew for their games on *Hockey Night in Canada*. Bud Poile, the team's first general manager, took me out fishing on a boat along with Babe Pratt, who was the team's assistant GM and was also in charge of community relations. The truth is, we didn't do any fishing; we just enjoyed a wonderful boat ride and drank a few beers and talked about *Hockey Night*.

Bud asked me, "Are you going to hire Babe for your crew? It would be important for us to have Babe on your show."

"I don't know," I said. I couldn't really commit at that point, although in the back of my mind I knew he'd be pretty good on television.

"Well, the way I see it, you've got two choices," Bud said. "You either hire him to be on *Hockey Night in Canada* from Vancouver, or we're going to throw you overboard."

"He's hired!"

Babe just loved being on *Hockey Night*, but I couldn't use him outside of Vancouver because of his association with the hockey team. There was also the risk that, if we used him in Edmonton or Calgary — which I would have loved to do — he might make comments that could be construed as derogatory about players in other organizations. That wouldn't have been acceptable.

Babe loved television and was a lovable ham. We did have to rein him in, though. His isolation truck was parked just inside the Pacific Coliseum, and after watching the game from all the isolated angles, he'd yell and scream — and even swear — at the Canucks players as they walked past. I finally had to tell him I didn't think it was good for *Hockey Night in Canada*, or for his team, to keep doing that. There wasn't usually anyone around to see or hear him, but you just never knew when somebody might show up, and it could be embarrassing for us.

Babe had been a Hall of Fame defenceman with the Maple Leafs and New York Rangers, and along with Danny Gallivan he became one of our show's greatest ambassadors. They would both go out and speak on our behalf to the sponsors and the public. Babe was a wonderful public speaker, and you couldn't be around him for long before he'd start spinning yarns from the past — and boy, was he funny.

He was a fun guy who didn't even mind poking fun at himself. The one story about Babe I've always enjoyed and will never forget involves the Toronto Maple Leafs, who had just lost the Stanley Cup. Babe was screening the Leafs' goalie, Turk Broda, and the puck went between his legs and into the net. Babe was sitting in the dressing room after the game, dejected about the outcome, when Conn Smythe came around to congratulate the players for their year.

Babe said, "Mr. Smythe, I'm sorry. I should have kept my legs closed."

Smythe looked at him and said, "Walter, your mother should have kept her legs closed."

Babe was a very entertaining analyst. He really understood the game, so it was vital that he pick his own highlights. He was with us for about a decade, but when Howie Meeker and Don Cherry got so popular, and once the Canucks began to earn a spot on the national telecasts, it was time for Babe to go. It was one thing in the early years, when Vancouver was an expansion team and wasn't getting into the playoffs, but once they became a contending team we didn't want to lose Cherry or Meeker simply because Vancouver was playing and we had to use Babe, who was not as well known across the rest of Canada.

If we hadn't found Don, and if Babe had been willing to quit his job with the Canucks, he might have grown into a similar role to the one Don took on. But that wasn't going to happen: he loved his team and his management job.

So, I called him and told him, "Babe, I've got bad news. We're moving forward and we're changing the show. I've got Cherry and Meeker. You've been a great guy for us, a true *Hockey Night in Canada* guy, but we have to let you go."

"Ralph, I've appreciated it," he said. "It has been great for me. It was a great thrill."

He had nothing but positive things to say about his experience with the show and added, "Listen: I'll keep my blue jacket, and if you ever need me, you can depend on me. I'll be there."

I always tried not to fall in love with the people who worked for me, because I knew there might come a day when I'd have to let them go. But it seemed the guys I liked were the guys I had to let go. And there was nobody I liked more than Babe Pratt.

Walter "Babe" Pratt died in the press box of the Pacific Coliseum on December 16, 1988, watching his beloved Canucks — an appropriate way to end a fabulous life in hockey. I miss you, Babe, and so do the fans in Vancouver.

HELEN HUTCHINSON THE GIRL OF WEDNESDAY NIGHT

The notion of hiring a woman for *Hockey Night in Canada* actually came from my boss, Ted Hough. He loved the idea of being an innovator, when it came to talent as well as on the technical side. In the early 1970s, Helen was the star of *Canada AM* and had won numerous awards. She was also a sports fan and had been married to a pro football star. There was no need for an audition — just a luncheon meeting, and she was hired to be on our Wednesday-night shows on CTV.

I liked her very much and loved her attitude and personality. Unfortunately, these sentiments were not shared by my team of talent — especially Dave Hodge, who saw her as encroaching on his territory.

I tried to personally protect Helen by giving her the choice interviews and film subjects, but our male-chauvinistic world wasn't ready for the idea of a woman on *HNiC.* The NHL players also rejected the idea, so it was really tough for Helen. Looking back, we were years ahead of our time. Today, there are many women in the media covering hockey. The idea would work today, because Helen was terrific and very professional.

I did my best, and Helen gave it her all, and our surveys showed that the audience liked her work. But after one season, we had to call it quits. I wanted her back, but she refused. She'd had enough.

Sorry, Helen; I was disappointed, too.

INTERMISSION
TWO HISTORIC
MATCHUPS

Chapter 10

A CLOSE CALL THE 1972 SUMMIT SERIES

> "That damned Esposito!" — Soviet coach Vsevolod Bobrov while being interviewed in Moscow in the summer of 1973

For me, the story of the 1972 Summit Series really begins in the summer leading up to the event — in Jamaica, of all places. Frank Selke, who was the vice-president of special events for *Hockey Night in Canada*, had asked me to join a number of NHL players in Jamaica for the opening of a new golf course that was being paid for by the Morgan Estates Company, a real-estate developer.

The deal was quite simple, really: during the day, we would golf with people who had bought property on the Iron Shores Golf Course, and then we had the evenings to ourselves. We brought our wives and kids, and Frank organized events to keep them entertained during the days. All in all, it was really a wonderful trip — and very revealing.

Naturally, the players who were invited were quality guys — people like Frank Mahovlich, Rod Seiling, Bobby Clarke and Paul Henderson. All of them were stars in the NHL at the time, though Clarke had only played in the league a few years. The last thing we needed was guys who were going to go there and get plastered during the day and makes fools of themselves. It was a classy group.

The golf was a great deal of fun, especially when we got the opportunity to tee it up with Doug Sanders, who won more than twenty tournaments on the PGA circuit. Our favourite times, though, were the evenings, when we would all gather at the beach for a few drinks. Without the sponsors and owners around, the guys felt free to relax a little. And every night the topic of conversation was the same: how they were going to kick the Russians' asses in the upcoming Summit Series.

The guys would sit there and say, "Just wait until those Russians see the Big M! They won't be able to stop him. Wait'll they see Kenny Dryden in goal. He'll shut them down for sure. We'll beat them in eight straight games!" The cockiness was a constant among this group.

"Listen," I would say. "I've seen these guys play at Olympics and other international events. They're good. Don't think they're not as good as you."

"What do you mean?" they'd scoff. Or they'd say, "You've got to be kidding." They were adamant that they were going to beat the Russians — kill them on the smaller North American ice surface — and nobody could convince them to the contrary. The conventional wisdom was that Canadians were the greatest hockey players in the world and that the Russians, who dominated international play, only did so because Canada never sent its best pros to the Olympics or World Championships. The Soviets were overrated — period!

The strange thing is, after a week of listening to them boast about how much better they were than the Russians, they actually had me believing it, too. Originally, I thought the series would turn out to be closer than the players did, but by the time I got home from this trip, there I was, telling everybody I talked to about how badly Canada was going to crush the Russians. I'd been converted! How could a team that boasted seven of the top ten scorers from the 1971–72 NHL season not steamroll these chumps? The only players missing from the top ten were Bobby Orr, whose chronically bad knee was on the fritz; Bobby Hull, who had jumped to the World Hockey Association (the decision had been made that only NHLers would represent Canada, and how foolish that seems today!); and Johnny Bucyk, who was in the twilight of his career and was passed over in favour of younger players.

The defence included Brad Park, a First Team NHL All-Star in '71–72 and the closest thing there was back then to Orr, along with Second Team All-Stars Bill White and Pat Stapleton. Montreal kingpins Serge Savard and Guy Lapointe rounded out the blue line corps. In net were future Hall of Famers Tony Esposito and Ken Dryden.

The amazing thing is that every guy who went on that golf trip made Team Canada. Clarke would say that he didn't think he had a shot at making the club because he felt he was too young. As it turned out, he was a pivotal player in the eight-game series. Henderson also doubted he would make the team.

Fast-forward to a few months later, as the players assembled in Toronto for training camp. My first impression of the players was that they didn't look to be in any better shape than when I saw them in Jamaica. You could instantly tell that they hadn't been training. Not only that, but the training camp was a joke. These guys simply weren't taking the Russians seriously, and boy, would that have severe consequences. Holding the training camp in Toronto was a huge mistake. The guys would skate a bit in the day and then whoop it up at night. The Canadian players would watch the Russians practice and they'd laugh at them. They were so decidedly arrogant. All the while, I had this lingering feeling that the poor training camp was going to come back to haunt the Canadians, and when it did, our players might be in for a real shock.

Well, we didn't have to wait long for that to happen.

The advance scouting on the Russians was also seriously flawed. And we would hear stories about how the Russian players would steal the soap out of the showers and take bread from banquets to give to their wives. They were very, very poor. It reinforced the idea that a Third World country was coming to play against the elite. What people often forget about the series is how politically charged it was. This was more than just a battle for hockey supremacy — it was capitalism versus communism; our way of life versus theirs. Phil

Esposito has said numerous times over the years that he would have killed to win that series.

On the night of September 2, seconds after the puck was dropped at centre ice at the Montreal Forum to begin Game 1, Phil Esposito carried it into the Russian zone along the right-hand side boards. The left-shooting centre who had led the NHL in scoring in three of the past four seasons suddenly switched hands, shooting right-handed at the Russian net. That demonstration summed up just how little the Canadians thought of their opponents.

Goalie Vladislav Tretiak easily stopped Esposito's weak shot, but thirty seconds into the game he wasn't as fortunate, when Espo popped a Frank Mahovlich rebound past the bewildered goaltender. Six minutes later, Henderson scored and the party was on. It seemed as though Canada would blow the Russians out of the water, just as the players had predicted on the beaches of Jamaica.

The Russians, though, had other ideas. Before the period ended, the fast-skating Soviets tied the game and then, with the only two goals of the middle frame, took a lead they would never relinquish. In the end, it was the Canadians who seemed puzzled and confused. The Russians would throw five-man units on the ice and had no reservations about carrying the puck back into their own zone to regroup if they ran into trouble at the Canadian blue line. They went to open ice. They had invented the two- and three-man forecheck and called it "flooding the zone." It's a common tactic in today's NHL game, but in 1972 we had never seen anything like it before. Their forwards weaved between centre and the wings, seemingly at will. After one game, Esposito came up to me and said, "That Yakushev who I'm playing against — is he a centre, a right winger or a left winger? I can't tell — he's all over the place."

At 8:32 of the third period, Clarke scored to make it 4–3 for the Russians, but they responded with three unanswered goals to win easily, 7–3. An entire nation watched in shock as their heroes, the best players in the world — or so they thought — were humbled and humiliated. One game, one stunning upset, changed hockey forever.

These Russians were good — damn good.

Nearly thirty-five years later, on January 29, 2007 — the night that his Number 29 was retired and raised to the rafters at the Bell Centre in Montreal — Team Canada goalie Ken Dryden said that Game 1 of the Summit Series was the worst night of his hockey career. I am certain there are many others who share that sentiment. After all, we were not supposed to lose a single game in this series, let alone the opener.

I saw some of the guys after the first game, and they were in shock. It was depressing.

Two nights later in Toronto, with Tony Esposito replacing Dryden in goal, Team Canada rebounded for a 4–1 win, outshooting the visitors 36–21. That game was highlighted by what was arguably the finest goal of the entire series. Peter Mahovlich grabbed the puck in Canada's zone, skated coast to coast through a host of checkers and deked Tretiak for a shorthanded tally early in the third period.

But even with the series tied, the Canadians knew they were in for a tough battle. The win in Game 2 was hardly the pasting they had expected to lay on the Russians before the series began. It was more of a relief than a message to the opposition.

By now, it was obvious to the Canadian players (and to the fans, for that matter) that they weren't in nearly as good physical condition as the Russians, who had banded together two months prior to the start of the series for intensive training. The Russians were taking the series quite seriously. Also, it was quickly apparent that many of the Russians were as good as, if not better than, many of the best Canadians. Suddenly, players such as Alexander Yakushev, Tretiak, Valeri Kharlamov and Yuri Liapkin, virtual unknowns to the Canadian players, were becoming household names.

After the teams played to a 4–4 tie on September 6 in Winnipeg, the Soviets regained the series lead two nights later with a convincing 5–3 victory at Vancouver's Pacific Coliseum. At the game's conclusion, a very frustrated and tired Phil Esposito was interviewed by Johnny Esaw and went on a now-famous rant about how disappointed he was that the team was being booed by the Vancouver crowd.

"To the people across Canada, we tried," Esposito said. "We gave it our best. To the people that booed us, geez, all of us guys are really disheartened. We're disillusioned and disappointed. We cannot believe the bad press we've got; the booing we've got in our own buildings."

"I'm completely disappointed. I cannot believe it. Every one of us guys — thirty-five guys — we came out because we love our country. Not for any other reason. We came because we love Canada."

Esaw was told numerous times through his headset to wrap up the interview, but to his credit he seized the moment, standing there and allowing Esposito to vent. He knew Espo was on a roll and that it was pure gold. It was a great journalistic moment.

The same players who had laughed at and mocked the Russians, who had treated the series as a joke, weren't laughing any longer. When we took off to Europe for the remaining four games of the event, it didn't look to me as if Canada had any hope of winning the series. They were physically and mentally out of it. And they hadn't even hit the hard part yet: playing in Moscow.

* * *

I worked on the Summit Series as the consulting producer, while Johnny Esaw of CTV and Gord Craig of the CBC were the actual producers. In truth, they didn't come to me and "consult" very much. That was fine by me. After all, the key people — directors Ron Harrison and Larry Brown as well as producers John Spalding and Ralph Abraham — were highly skilled and well trained, and they essentially followed the *Hockey Night in Canada* template. And at least in Canada, the arenas and facilities were familiar to us.

But although I might have been there as a figurehead, I learned a lot in that series. There were some striking differences in the way the Russians approached the broadcasts. For instance, by this time, the two-man booth, with a play-by-play man and a colour commentator, was a staple of North American sports coverage. But the Soviets had only one announcer, Nikolai Ozerov. And rather than call the action from the booth, he would situate himself on the bench, alongside the players. Lately, North American broadcasters have begun putting an analyst at ice level, but it was unheard of back then.

Soviet television didn't produce a pre-game show, either. They'd go on the air just as the puck was about to be dropped, and during the intermission they'd show a blank screen with music playing. And when the game ended, the picture faded to black; Ozerov didn't wrap up, and they didn't broadcast the player handshakes or the presentations of awards. It was simply game over.

When the series switched to Moscow, we used the feed from Soviet television, and it wasn't anywhere near what we were used to in Canada. For instance, the cameras delivered wider shots than you would ever see on *Hockey Night in Canada* — and the close-ups weren't close enough. Maybe the wider rink accounted for this difference. They had a few microphones aimed at the ice, but they didn't come close to picking up the sounds of the game the way we did on *HNiC* — everything was very muffled, and you couldn't hear the sticks hitting the puck. That trip really showed us how far ahead North American television was in 1972, especially in terms of sports coverage. Of course, there was no way we could even consider teaching them how to do things our way — that would have been an insult.

We brought three of our own cameras to the Luzhniki Ice Palace, to make sure we captured some of what the Soviet feed ignored. One camera was pointed at the Team Canada bench, which was fortunate because the Russians didn't aim their cameras that way too often. While Ozerov called the game from ice level, our announcers sat in the press box, just as they did back home, but it was a tight squeeze and very hot in there. Fortunately, Bob Cole and Foster Hewitt were able to sit far enough apart that they weren't stepping over each other's broadcast.

To the Soviets, the series was like an arts exchange, an exercise in diplomacy. So it was no good to bitch and moan about the conditions. The good news is that the games were so good, and there was so much passion surrounding the series, that I don't think anyone really noticed the lack of sophistication of the Russian feed. And on a personal note, the series provided one of the great thrills of my career: my younger brother, Jim, was the floor manager, working with Foster Hewitt and Brian Conacher. I was very proud of him, and it gave us a chance to spend some time together.

* * *

Between Games 4 and 5, Canada had a stopover in Stockholm, Sweden, for a pair of exhibition games against the Swedish national team. Canada wanted to use the games to get used to playing on the larger European ice surfaces. The team also faced a crisis. Some of the players who hadn't played at all or had been used only sparingly were upset and decided to return to Canada. Among those who left was veteran Vic Hadfield, the New York Ranger who had finished fourth in NHL scoring the year before and was upset that younger players were getting the nod ahead of him. He was embarrassed at not playing when he felt he could help the team. The others included youngsters Jocelyn Guevremont, Richard Martin and Gilbert Perreault. To me, of all those who went home, Perreault was the one who probably should have received more playing time. He had a goal and an assist in two games and was one Canadian who could not only keep up with the swift Russians, but could outskate most of them.

Being away from their wives and families had its advantages for a team trying desperately to bond. And now that the malcontents had departed the scene, those who remained could get down to the task at hand.

Our arrival in Moscow was like nothing I had ever experienced before in my life. We were kept on the bus for more than ninety minutes while soldiers went through our belongings, taking with them our beer and steaks. If the Canadian players weren't already paranoid enough being on communist turf for the first time in most of their lives, this certainly wasn't helping matters.

Everywhere you went, there were soldiers. To be truthful, though, I think I enjoyed this part of the trip more than the players. I had travelled more than most of them in my career, and the experience of going to different places in the world was delightful. The players didn't care about going to the opera or circus the way I did; all they cared about was the hockey. Given the fact that their grip on hockey supremacy was slipping between their fingers, I was not surprised.

To me, Game 5 was a crucial turning point. Although Canada lost 5–4 — thanks largely to absolutely horrible officiating — it was the final straw for Team Canada. There would be no more losing. They were no longer in it for their country, for Canada. They were in it for themselves, and perhaps for the 3,000 or so brave fans who made the journey with them. Funny, we all felt so alone in Moscow — the players, the press and the fans.

Three things happened after that game. First, the Russians assumed the same arrogance the Canadians had displayed before Game 1. Suddenly, *they* were the cocky ones. You could see in their practices; it was as if they were now thinking, "We're going to kill these guys. We can't be beaten by these Canadians." And I think that swagger got under our guys' skins. Second, our guys were finally getting in shape. The twenty-second huff-and-puff shifts were turning into high-energy forty-second shifts. And finally, I was seeing signs of good old-fashioned Canadian heart and tenacity. The players would bend, but they would not break.

I had never seen Paul Henderson so intense. I had known him for quite some time, and that was not his style. Back then, he used to like to have a few drinks and have fun. He was cheery and fun-loving. But after Game 5, all he — and many of his teammates — did was growl.

Even the press caught the fever. Some of the best sports reporters Canada has ever known had made the trip — people like Trent Frayne, Jim Coleman, Jim Hunt, Red Fisher. They were real pros and competitors, but suddenly even they were showing signs of being pro-Canada. I'd never seen togetherness in the media like that before and I never saw it again.

Good coaching won this series. Prior to Game 6, Team Canada assistant coach John Ferguson told me that Canada had a new strategy. He and head coach Harry Sinden came up with the idea of beating the zone press by having Canada's players shoot the puck around the boards to open ice, thus trapping the Soviet forwards deep. When they started doing that, suddenly it was Canada that was getting the two-on-ones and three-on-twos; now it was the Russians chasing the Canadians, instead of the other way around. Canada started to dominate the play. I give the Team Canada coaching staff credit for having the foresight to make the required changes and, above all else, for keeping their cool.

All the scoring in Game 6 came in the second period, the Russians scoring first and last while Canada netted three in a row in between. Henderson had what proved to be the game-winner at 6:36.

The pattern continued of Canadians being called by the referee for just about everything they did while the Russians got away with murder. The most memorable call against Canada, however, was deserved. Clarke, with just a little nudging from Ferguson, gave Kharlamov a wicked two-hander across the ankle and was rewarded with a slashing minor and a ten-minute misconduct. Kharlamov missed Game 7 and was ineffective in Game 8.

Now, there are those who have suggested over the years that Clarke effectively removed Russia's best player from the series. That was not the case. In my opinion, Yakushev, who finished the series with a team-leading 7 goals and 11 points, was the Soviets' best player. Right-winger Boris Mikhailov, who had 3 goals and 5 points, was also better than Kharlamov.

After six games, the Soviets had won three and Canada had won two, with one tie. The Russians were scrambling, praying for help from extremely biased officials. Meanwhile, we — by which, of course, I mean Canada — had momentum. The other thing we had was the greatest show of leadership I have ever witnessed in hockey, on the part of Phil Esposito. It was the only time I have seen a player take a team and carry it on his back.

Espo scored two goals in Canada's 4–3 win in Game 7, in which Henderson was once again fortunate enough to supply the winning goal. Canada needed a victory in Game 8 to claim the series. The Russians contended that if the game ended in a tie, they would be the series champs on the grounds that they would have outscored Canada over the eight games.

Although Tony Esposito had been in goal for Game 7, it was decided that Dryden would start in the finale, a decision that left many in Canada watching the game with their fingers crossed. Needless to say, the game was a nail-biter, and when the Russians pulled ahead 5–3 after forty minutes, I distinctly recall saying, "We've got to get the next goal or we're dead."

Phil Esposito went out and got it before the third period was three minutes old. To me, Phil's goal was so important. Had the Russians scored first in the third period, I don't believe the Canadians could have climbed back into the contest. I don't think there was a hockey player alive who could have led his team the way Esposito did. The message he sent was along the lines of "I'm going to do it. If you guys don't want to do it, fuck you! I'm going to do it." Every inch of him was there to win.

Years later, when I filmed the series *Summit on Ice*, Phil told me, "This was not hockey to me; this was war. I would have killed those guys. I would have killed the referees."

The best thing that the Summit Series did for us was to put Canada's tenacity under the spotlight. As Espo said, "You can lose the Stanley Cup and still show your face. But we could not lose this series."

Yvan Cournoyer tied the score at 12:56, and now the only thing left was for Henderson to score the game-winner for the third game in a row. He did exactly that at 19:26.

Henderson told me that, as he sat on the bench in the final minute, he had a premonition and did something he claims he had never done before or after: he shouted for a teammate to leave the ice so he could go on. It wasn't his line or his shift, but it was his *time*.

Foster Hewitt called the action for the millions who were at home watching our broadcast on television: "Here's a shot. Henderson made a wild stab for it and fell. Here's another shot. Right in front. They score! Henderson has scored for Canada!"

Canadians breathed a huge sigh of relief. Team Canada had retained bragging rights for our country, though not in the easy fashion they imagined they would. The victory set off a wild celebration amongst those of us in Russia — the media and the fans. Or were we all fans?

After the game, I went into the dressing room and saw Henderson sitting in his stall, virtually motionless. It was as if he had been shot through the heart — he was so emotionally drained.

I tried to speak to him, but it was as if he didn't hear me … as if he didn't know who I was. I had never seen such a beaten-down guy in my life. He had left it all out on the ice.

Years later, when we went back to Russia to revisit the series, Henderson told me, "Ralph, I knew I was going to score that goal." As he told me, he cried. It was still such an emotional experience for him.

That was before he found the Lord. Maybe that's *why* he later found the Lord and became a minister.

Back at the media hotel, we celebrated the victory, partying as if we were the ones who had won the event. I can remember leading a train of people around a ballroom, singing loudly (to the tune of the Russian national anthem): "Phil Esposito and Tony Esposito, Phil Esposito, Tony Esposito…"

I looked behind me and, fuelled by beer and spirits, there was the cream of the crop of hockey writers in Canada, dancing right along with me. It was a glorious sight to behold. On this night they were not reporters; they were all Canadians.

I must say that Canada would not have won the Summit Series without the leadership, guidance and determination of Alan Eagleson. I know he has had a lot of problems since, including being booted out of the Hockey Hall of Fame for wrongdoings as head of the NHL Players' Association, but Eagleson was a tower of strength for Team Canada, standing up to the Russians at every turn. We could not have won without Al. It was his shining moment.

If not for him, the Russians would have run roughshod over the Canadians in the final four games. Every time they tried to put the screws to Team Canada, the Eagle was there with his chest puffed out to turn them away. They changed Canada's practice times, schedules — even tried to change the on-ice officials — but Al stood steadfast. Nobody had his guts and fortitude.

In Game 8, when the goal judge failed to turn on the red light after Cournoyer tied the score at five, Eagleson went berserk. He immediately darted from his seat, on the opposite side of the rink from Canada's bench, but was quickly roughed up by the military police. Seeing the squabble, some members of Team Canada left the bench to come to the aid of their leader. They escorted Eagleson across the ice and back to their bench, where he watched the remainder of the game.

If you watch highlights of the series today, you will see Al hiking up his pants and straightening his jacket as he goes across the ice. He later told me it was because his mom told him to always be presentable in public.

This is one of those cases where having a few of our own cameras in the Ice Palace really paid off. We were able to zoom in for a close-up look at the fracas. It was a hand-held camera that captured Eagleson being brought to the bench by Canadian players. Meanwhile, Soviet television stayed with a wide-angle shot.

Team Canada received a hero's welcome upon returning to Canada. One thing I'll never forget is Serge Savard pinching a stick that John Ferguson had had autographed by the members of both teams and giving it to Prime Minister Pierre Trudeau after the players got off the plane in Ottawa. Ferguson — who figured that the stick would be of historical value — couldn't leave the plane under his own power and didn't find out about Serge's unauthorized gift until later. Shortly afterwards, Eagleson contacted the Prime Minister (who really wasn't a hockey fan) and got the stick back for his pal. What a guy.

I was proud to be a part of the Summit Series. When we went back the following year to tell the Russians' side of the story of the series (a trip paid for by Hockey Canada), I interviewed many of the Russian players and their coach, Vsevolod Bobrov.

Bobrov said, "We had it planned perfectly. We never should have lost." He said his players were in great shape; they were like iron. And he told me that, when he knew Canadian scouts were in attendance before the series started, the Russians would never use the zone press — or, as he called it, "flooding the zone" — that was to confuse the Canadians early in the series. Through a translator, he said, "We felt the Canadian strength was also their weakness — that was their emotion. We felt the Canadians would become too emotional and take lots of penalties. After four games in Canada we were positive we were right. But that damned Esposito…"

And he stopped.

Chapter 11

THE MIRACLE ON ICE THE 1980 U.S. OLYMPIC TEAM

"Well, one thing we've learned here is there is no story with the USA hockey team." — Roone Arledge, head of ABC Sports, after watching Team USA get blown out in a pre-Olympic exhibition game against the Soviet Union

Today, more than a quarter of a century later, it remains arguably the greatest sports story in history — a bunch of college kids who stunned the world by capturing the gold medal in hockey at the 1980 Winter Olympics. But to say that I expected to witness such a historic achievement would be the farthest thing from the truth. To me, the thirteenth Winter Games shaped up to be "just another Olympics."

I was producing for ABC, having directed their coverage at Innsbruck in 1976, and had gone early to Lake Placid, New York, to make sure everything was in order. To repeat, there was no "buzz" around the hockey tournament, mainly because nobody in the world imagined that anybody would come close to the powerful Soviet squad, loaded down with such superstars as Vladislav Tretiak, Boris Mikhailov, Vladimir Krutov and Sergei Makarov. Simply put, it was the best Soviet team in history.

A bunch of us — including Ken Dryden, who was going to be ABC's hockey analyst, director Ron Harrison and the veteran host Jim McKay — gathered at the broadcast centre to watch the Russians play the U.S. at Madison Square Garden in a February 9 tune-up game. It was a disaster for the Americans! The Russians skated circles around them, humiliating them 10–3. I think the Soviets could have scored ten more goals, but they held back to avoid embarrassing their opponents. The Americans were awful.

We couldn't believe it. Roone Arledge, who *was* ABC Sports at the time, got up and left after the second period. The network had invested millions of dollars in its Olympic hockey coverage and was banking on the U.S. team to give them a big story. Before Arledge departed, he left us with this little nugget: "Well, one thing we've learned here is there's no story with the USA hockey team."

And the fact is, we all agreed with him. After all, this was the Soviet team that had beaten the NHL's best players in the 1979 Challenge Cup, and many of them had been on the 1972 squad that gave Team Canada a run for its money.

Still, we had a job to do. ABC had assembled a very good team. The production crew was mostly Canadian, and we had ten cameras in the arena. Dryden, the recently retired Hall of Fame goaltender for the Montreal Canadiens, was to be the analyst, while thirty-five-year-old Al Michaels was set to call the play-by-play. Despite his youth, Michaels had already made at least one memorable call in his broadcasting career: in 1972, he announced Johnny Bench's game-tying homer in the bottom of the ninth inning of the final game of the National League playoffs against Pittsburgh (the Reds went on to the World Series after George Foster scored on a wild pitch). Before the Games, I gave Michaels a few tips here and there, telling him when to talk and when to let the analyst do his thing. Dryden, who is known for his gift of the gab, had no problem talking. He would break down the play and describe what the USA was doing right or wrong ... and it only took him hours to say it. He could overanalyze a two-car funeral.

Actually, if you watch the tape of Mike Eruzione's winning goal in the game against the Russians, Dryden is talking over Michaels, still analyzing the game. But I'm getting ahead of myself.

The tournament began with very little fanfare; ABC no longer gave a crap about the hockey, as speed skater Eric Heiden had become the focal point. A few weeks before the Olympics, he had broken a couple of world records, and he was on the verge of winning an unprecedented five Olympic gold medals, breaking four Olympic records and another world record in the process. There were also hopes for the U.S. ski team led by Phil Mahre.

The Americans opened the tournament with a 2–2 tie against Sweden, followed by a 7–3 defeat of Czechoslovakia. Meanwhile, the Soviets were blowing away their first two opponents, and there could be no question they would win the gold medal. Arledge asked us to get some footage of the Russians, so we taped the 16–0 laugher over Japan. The Japanese were the worst hockey team I had ever seen. The Soviets led 12–0 after the first period and treated the final forty minutes as a practice — they rarely shot, preferring to work on their passing.

I had hired a couple of Canadian kids, Jim Nill (now the assistant general manager of the Detroit Red Wings) and Cary Farelli, to works as spotters on our broadcasts. Both were surprise late cuts from Team Canada and were going to be sent home, so I gave them jobs, which allowed them to stay in Lake Placid. They would watch the games to look for things the announcers might miss. Nill and Farelli were laughing their heads off as they watched the Japanese players chasing the Russians all over the ice. It may well have been the funniest hockey game in Olympic history.

The Russians also beat the Netherlands, 17–4, and Poland by an 8–1 score. They were undefeated in the preliminary round. But the United States had also made it into the medal round, defeating Norway, West Germany and Romania without much trouble. Very quietly, their performance was developing into a story after all. Not that the U.S. team was much help in telling that story — their coach,

Herb Brooks, was an absolute ass with the media. He wouldn't allow us into practices and wouldn't grant us access to his players.

In the meantime, we were really having a joyful time at the Olympics, with ABC picking up the tab and sparing no expense. The meals were especially memorable. One evening, Arledge came into our hotel with his daughter, hoping to have dinner. There were so many people in the dining room that it looked as if it was going to take forever for him to be served. He fixed the problem — he "bought" the dining room for the duration of the Olympics. ABC people occupied most of the hotel rooms anyway, so he figured, why not?

"We have the rest of the hotel, we may as well have the dining room," Arledge told me.

The network provided me with a car during the Olympics, but I didn't use it. I enjoyed walking to the rink each day. Our hotel was at one end of town, and the rink at the other. It was a beautiful walk — and besides, the traffic was awful on Main Street.

The way the medal round worked in the tournament, the Americans and Swedes, as the leaders of the "Blue" division, each had to play the Soviets and Finns, the two qualifiers from the "Red" division. The Soviets' 4–2 defeat of Finland in the preliminary round counted in the medal standings, as did the 2–2 tie between the Americans and the Swedes. There was a little bit of talk about the Americans' chances and their unbeaten record in the preliminary games, but nobody was giving them a hope in hell against the Russians — including the hockey crew.

On the night before the big game, Dryden, Harrison, Michaels and I went out to dinner. It was the first time we ate away from our hotel. We were having a grand time, and I'll never forget Michaels saying, "If we [the U.S.] ever won this game, it'd be huge!"

But none of the rest of us thought the Americans had a chance. Even Ken Dryden said the network "had better put us on early while the United States is still in the game."

Michaels wouldn't have any of it. "You guys are all so negative," he said. "If we win this game, I'm going to say, 'It's the greatest miracle in sports history.'"

I looked at him and pleaded, "Al, don't say something like that. That's corny."

No sooner had I said that than Chet Forte, who was a senior producer at ABC (best known for his work on *Monday Night Football*), came into the restaurant and dropped a bombshell: the game would be broadcast live around the world (at 5 p.m. Eastern time), but it would be aired on a tape-delayed basis in prime time in the United States.

I was incredulous. "What? This is stupid! I'll bet CTV is going to show the game live across Canada."

We were all pissed off. Here was the most significant game of the tournament for the American team, and it wasn't going to be shown live in the United States. But then we realized why — the U.S. were expected to be blown away by the Russians, so it didn't make a lot of sense politically to get the affiliates upset by pre-empting dinner-hour newscasts and other money-making shows that local stations showed in the early-evening time slots.

The next morning, I was walking down Main Street to the arena, when a limousine decked out with two Soviet flags pulled up alongside of me. The head of Soviet television, Enricus Yuskavetdez, was in the car. He stopped and rolled down his window.

"Ralph Mellanby! Jump in and I'll give you a ride to the arena."

"Are you nuts?" I replied. "That's the last car I'd get into!" People were all over Main Street, and I'd hate to been seen getting into an official Soviet car. I said, "I'll see you later and we'll have a beer." He seemed embarrassed, as he had been my pal since 1972.

Prior to the game against the Russians, I had my pre-game meeting with the crew and told them that the main thing was to be careful with their shots and to remember that we were following a storyline, which was U.S. goalie Jim Craig and his father in the stands. ABC was highlighting the fact that Craig's mother had died of cancer just before the Olympics. We therefore needed to be sure to get some shots of his father.

I had an excellent crew working with me; the bigger the assignment, the better they performed. Now the biggest moment had arrived, so off we went. But I'll never forget that there was no excitement among the crew. To them, it was just another game, another job.

The Russians scored first, as expected, but then the Americans tied it. Now the storyline was building. The Russians should have been up by five goals in the second period — they were outplaying the Americans that badly. But the Americans were hanging tight. On one play, Valeri Kharlamov deked Craig, had a wide-open net and flipped the puck up — only to hit the crossbar. Never before or since have I seen a Russian team miss so many chances.

Suddenly, one of my spotters told me that the Russians had pulled Tretiak and replaced him with the backup goalie, Vladimir Myshkin.

"What?" I couldn't believe it. Tretiak had never been pulled — and was never again pulled in his career! We got a shot of the coach, Viktor Tikhonov, and a shot of Tretiak on the bench.

The Russians continued to pile up the scoring chances (they outshot the Americans 39–16 in the game), but with no luck. Eight and a half minutes into the third period, the USA tied it at 3–3, and we got a shot of Brooks at the bench. Even he looked like he was in shock! The look on his face is still etched in my mind today.

When Mike Eruzione scored the game-winner for the Americans with ten minutes remaining in the game, the arena went nuts. The phone in my truck rang, and it was Chet Forte.

"Ralph, make sure we get Brooks if anything happens."

I said, "Hey, I know what you want. You want a shot of [Craig's] father, right?"

This was now perhaps the biggest story in the history of sports in the U.S. And the whole truck seemed to freeze up. Everybody on our crew tightened up. I had to urge the guys on like a coach — "Just keep doing the job, guys. The main thing at the end of the game is to make sure we get the right shots."

Ken Dryden ended up doing a fine job as analyst, having mastered the art of short stories. And thank God Al Michaels didn't listen to me at dinner — his call of Eruzione's goal ("Do you believe in miracles?

Yes!") has gone down in broadcasting history.

We went back to the ABC lounge to watch the game in prime time, and everybody was wearing ear-to-ear smiles.

Two days later, the U.S. were to play Finland with a gold medal on the line. This time, the game would be carried live, and it was all but guaranteed that our broadcast would be seen by a record audience for a hockey game. Beforehand, I told the crew to focus on their jobs. "Stay out of the bars and be on top of your game ... and quit chasing skirts." I told them I'd provide them with beer outside the truck after the game as a reward (a promise I made good on).

The Americans secured the gold medal — and a place in history — with a 4–2 victory over the Finns (imagine the reaction if they had lost?). When the game ended, there was bedlam. We were looking all over the arena, but couldn't find goaltender Jim Craig. "Where the fuck is he?" we were screaming in the truck. We got a shot of his dad in the stands, but we couldn't find the son — and he was *the* story of the Olympics.

What we didn't know yet was that one of our cameramen, Al Mountford, had spotted Craig going over to the bench, yelling, "Where's my father? Where's my father?" and then finding him. The "iso" guys (the technicians who watched the feeds from the isolation cameras to grab shots for replays) captured it on tape. All we knew was that Craig had left the ice and we'd missed the defining moment of the entire Winter Games.

The place was still a madhouse when Mountford yelled over the intercom that he thought he might have gotten the shot earlier on tape. We had it! Thirty seconds later, I instructed director Ron Harrison to take a wide shot of the celebration on the ice. Then we cut to the tape, and you couldn't tell the difference — it looked like a live shot. Strictly speaking, we fudged it, and in doing so we were taking a massive risk. In those days, there were FCC regulations that prohibited taped material from being cut into a live feed. But this was history.

The next thing I knew, Arledge was calling me on my headset.

"Great shot, Ralph! That's the shot of the Lake Placid Games!"

He didn't know it was on tape, and I wasn't about to tell him. And when I got the crew together for beers after the game, I made them swear never to tell *anyone* how it had happened. Nobody ever spilled the beans about the delay, and that shot won Ron and me two Emmy Awards.

It is worth noting that, while the Americans arrived at the tournament as virtual unknowns, many of them went on to have successful NHL careers. Defenceman Ken Morrow, for example, joined the New York Islanders and became the first player ever to win an Olympic gold medal and the Stanley Cup in the same season. All told, Morrow won four Cups with the Islanders. Centre Neal Broten also won the Cup, with the New Jersey Devils, while the likes of Mike Ramsey, Dave Christian, Mark Johnson, Dave Silk, Steve Christoff, Mark Pavelich and Jack O'Callahan enjoyed various degrees of success in the NHL.

Eruzione, the Olympic hero with the winning goal who had had minor-pro experience prior to the Olympics, never played an NHL game. And Craig, who was so superb for the Americans in goal, played just 30 NHL games with Boston, Atlanta and Minnesota.

On a personal note, there is one funny anecdote about Lake Placid that I treasure. When I arrived at the Olympics, I was pleased to run into my friend Stuart Goodman. He had been an actor, and we used to room together in Montreal in the early '60s. I didn't know who my crew was going to be, but Stuart told me it included the top hand-held camera operator in the business. That turned out to be Stuart.

I put him in the penalty-box area because I knew he could do a lot with that camera from that location. The International Olympic Committee and the International Ice Hockey Federation had a rule: no cameramen on the ice at any time, for security reasons. I had covered the Olympics a number of times and I knew the rules, but apparently Stuart didn't. Or perhaps he simply didn't care.

Well, when the U.S. won the game against Russia, Stuart jumped on the ice and got some amazing shots. I was pleased, but I got in trouble afterwards from the IOC. Roone Arledge was called as well. It was a real piss-up.

I told Stuart, "You're not allowed to do that. You nearly had your credentials taken away. If it hadn't been for Roone, you'd be gone." "Yeah, yeah, yeah," he replied. "It won't happen again, but weren't the shots great!"

Well, when the United States won the gold medal against Finland, there he was, on the ice again. He just couldn't resist!

Later, he told me, "It's the last game. Hockey is over. I'm outta here. What are they going to do to me — pull my credentials?"

Stuart was right, of course. He's now one of the top feature-film and documentary producers in America. One day he'll win an Academy Award. I love him.

In 1987, I was in Calgary having dinner with Arledge as he was preparing for his final Olympics. He told me a secret — that ABC had insisted that CTV get me to run the host broadcaster production, "no matter what!"

I said, "Roone, you are my hero, but here's a secret that you won't like. I'm going to tell you something that you don't know, but forty of your crew know."

He looked startled.

I said, "You know that shot I won the Emmy for?"

"Yeah, that's one of the greatest shots in ABC Sports' history — Craig going, 'Where's my father? Where's my father?' What drama!"

I said, "That shot was taped thirty seconds earlier and we put it on the air as if it was live."

He said, "You're shitting me!" (And Roone didn't often swear.)

I assured him I wasn't, and I told him the whole story.

He looked at me and said, "Thank God you did it, Ralph — it's still the signature shot of the Olympics." Then he looked at me and said, "Boy, I'm glad you're a Canadian. No American producer would have done that."

As I look back on all the Olympic hockey I have produced and directed, the 1980 tournament was the absolute highlight.

Four years later, in Sarajevo, Mike Eruzione was hired by ABC as an analyst and we had dinner together. I told him how much I'd enjoyed the experience in Lake Placid and he said, "Ralph, if we had played them 100 more games, they would have won every game. But all the chances they missed — and the breaks … you know, it really was a 'miracle' that we could have beaten them. It was our time, our place. It will never happen again."

I agree — and it was a miracle in itself that we had "the shot," even if it was tape-delayed.

Ralph with Don Cherry and Wayne Gretzky during the premiere edition of
Don Cherry's Grapevine Show. —*courtesy* Don Cherry's Grapevine Show

Bobby Hull, Bobby Orr and Ralph
during taping of *Hockey Legends* in
Jamaica. —*Ralph Mellanby Collection*

Bobby Orr and Ralph at
Hockey Legends in Jamaica.
—*Ralph Mellanby Collection*

Paul Henderson and Bobby Orr with Ralph during taping of *Hockey Legends* in Jamaica. —*Ralph Mellanby Collection*

Ralph and Red Storey at *Hockey Legends* in Jamaica. —*Ralph Mellanby Collection*

CTV publicity photo of
Ralph for the 1988
Olympics in Calgary.
—*Ralph Mellanby Collection*

Hockey Night in Canada No-Stars Softball
Team. —*Ralph Mellanby Collection*

Hockey Night in Canada Legends at Hockey Night in Canada Golf
Tournament — Foster Hewitt, Bill Hewitt, Brian McFarlane, Ralph, Jack
Dennett, Bob Goldham and Ward Cornell. —*Ralph Mellanby Collection*

Jim Grattan, Film Camerman *Hockey Night in Canada*, Dan Kelly, Jean Beliveau, John Miller, Film Editor *Hockey Night in Canada* with the Stanley Cup. —*Ralph Mellanby Collection*

Glen Sather and Ralph at NHL Awards 1985. —*Ralph Mellanby Collection*

Ralph with Howie Meeker during *Hockey Pro Tips.* —*courtesy* Hokey Pro Tips

Frank Selke and Ralph at Maple Leaf Gardens circa 1967. —*courtesy* Hockey Night in Canada *(Canadian Sports Network)*

J.B. Chardola, Technical Producer and Ralph in the truck during a *Hockey Night in Canada* broadcast. —*courtesy* Hockey Night in Canada *(Canadian Sports Network)*

Ralph with Howie Meeker during *Hockey Pro Tips*. —*courtesy* Hokey Pro Tips

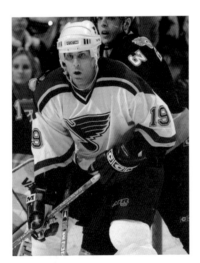

Scott Mellanby as a member
of the St. Louis Blues. —*courtesy*
St. Louis Blues

Publicity photo for *Hockey Night
in Canada* of Danny Gallivan, Gilles
Tremblay, Dick Irvin and Ralph.
—*courtesy* Hockey Night in Canada
(Canadian Sports Network)

Ralph with son Scott in Calgary. —
Ralph Mellanby Collection

Ralph with his first Emmy Award in
Los Angeles as the Host Broadcast
operation at the Olympic Winter
Games in Calgary 1988. —*courtesy ABC*

Publicity photo of Ralph. —*Ralph
Mellanby Collection*

George Gross and Ralph at Conn
Smythe Dinner. —*Ralph Mellanby Collection*

Ralph with Gordie Howe giving his agent, Jerry Patterson one of his famous elbows. —*Ralph Mellanby Collection*

Vladislav Tretiak and Ralph in Russia in 1991. —*Ralph Mellanby Collection*

Ken McKenzie, Publisher and Founder of Hockey News, Ralph, Punch Imlach, Bill Hewitt, John Anderson at Maple Leaf Gardens circa 1967. —*courtesy* Hockey Night in Canada *(Canadian Sports Network)*

Ralph with Gilles Tremblay, legendary Hockey Hall of Fame Broadcaster for *La Soiree du Hockey*, the French version of *Hockey Night in Canada* at a golf tournament. Ralph is wearing an ABC jacket which displeased his boss.

—*Ralph Mellanby Collection*

Rod Gilbert, star of the New York Rangers and Ralph at Studio 54 in New York. —*Ralph Mellanby Collection*

King Clancy, Ralph, Harold Ballard. —*Ralph Mellanby Collection*

Scott Mellanby at Henry Carr
Crusaders Junior B team practice.
—*Ralph Mellanby Collection*

Ralph with Alan Eagleson at NHL
Awards. —*Ralph Mellanby Collection*

Bobby Clarke, Janet Mellanby and Ralph at NHL Players Association
meetings in the Bahamas. —*Ralph Mellanby Collection*

Jim Grattan, Ralph, Brian McFarlane and Eddie Shack in Los Angeles filming the Eddie Shack Story.. —*Ralph Mellanby Collection*

Ralph with Maurice "Rocket" Richard at taping of *Don Cherry's Grapevine Show.*
—*courtesy* Don Cherry's Grapevine Show

Ralph and Red Storey.
—*Ralph Mellanby Collection*

Ralph and Bobby Clarke in a
publicity photo for *Showdown*.
—*courtesy of Paul Palmer, creator of* Showdown

Larry Robinson and Guy Lafleur
with Ralph in a publicity photo for
Showdown. —*courtesy of Paul Palmer,
creator of* Showdown

Ralph instructing the players participating in *Showdown*. —*courtesy of Paul Palmer,
creator of* Showdown

Danny Grant, Ralph and Darryl Sittler, Toronto Maple Leafs during taping of *Showdown*. —*courtesy of Paul Palmer, creator of* Showdown

Phil Esposito with Ralph during taping of the first *Showdown*.
—*courtesy of Paul Palmer, creator of* Showdown

Doug Favell and Ralph during the first *Showdown*. —*courtesy of Paul Palmer, creator of* Showdown

Frank Mahovlich and Ralph after another game of tennis.
—Ralph Mellanby Collection

Bobby Orr with Ralph during the *Hockey Legends* in Jamaica.
—Ralph Mellanby Collection

Bill Hewitt and Ralph on the golf course. —*Ralph Mellanby Collection*

Johnny Bucyk and Ralph during taping of *Hockey Legends* in Jamaica. —*Ralph Mellanby Collection*

Ralph with Dave Christian, Winnipeg Jets, Kevin McCarthy, Vancouver Canucks, Larry Robinson, Montreal Canadiens and Ralph during taping of *Hockey Pro Tips.* —*ccourtesy* Hockey Pro Tips

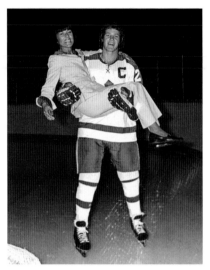

Hockey Night in Canada publicity photo of Helen Hutchison, the first female announcer on *Hockey Night in Canada* with Darryl Sittler. —*courtesy* Hockey Night in Canada *(Canadian Sports Network)*

Scott Mellanby. —*Ralph Mellanby Collection*

Ralph, Frank Selke, Dick Beddoes at NHL meetings. —*Ralph Mellanby Collection*

PART II
ON THE ICE

Chapter 12

THE COMPETITOR
TED LINDSAY

> "Lindsay was a pain in the ass to play against. I hated him, but boy, I wish he would have been a Canadien."
> — Bernie "Boom Boom" Geoffrion

Before my family moved to the farm in Essex, we lived in Windsor, and during the winter of 1946 I was invited to play in the annual "patrol boys hockey game" at the Windsor Arena. It was a big deal, a thrill. Each school had patrol boys — they were similar to what we'd call crossing guards today, except kids got to do it and it was considered an honour — and the game featured two teams, one from east Windsor and the other from west Windsor.

What made the game more memorable for me than anything else was the fact that I was twelve years old and captain of the East Windsor team, and therefore I got to take part in the opening ceremonial faceoff — for which the great Ted Lindsay of the Detroit Red Wings dropped the puck. What an awesome feeling it was for a young boy to be in the presence of a great NHLer. It may sound funny, but I distinctly remember Lindsay, who was in the second year of his NHL career, wearing a beautiful sweater. I mentioned the game to Ted years later, and he remembered being in attendance. Astounding!

Terrible Ted Lindsay — that's what he was called, because he was such a ferocious competitor who lived a tough life on and off the ice. Lindsay lost two wives and had his share of business deals go sour on

131

him, but even to this day you rarely see the man without a smile on his face.

Which is in direct conflict with the look on his face when he played hockey. He was like two people — Jekyll and Hyde, if you will. At five foot eight and 163 pounds, he was one of the smallest players in the league, but he was as tough as nails. There wasn't a player Lindsay wouldn't stand up to, and he'd drop the gloves with anybody — or use his stick on them. And that made him feared around the league. Old players used to tell me they hated playing against Lindsay because he wanted to win at all costs. He would hack and slash anybody to get the puck. Lindsay finished with more than 100 penalty minutes ten times in his seventeen-year NHL career — including in 1964–65, when he returned to action after a four-year retirement and had a whopping 173 penalty minutes.

Ted is very bitter about the way he was treated by Detroit coach and GM Jack Adams. Of course, a lot of that had to do with the fact that Lindsay was one of the first players to talk openly about starting a players' association. He was one of the driving forces behind the formation of the NHL Players' Association because he felt the owners were taking advantage of the players and spoke out against it. He was right, but in those days it was dangerous to be outspoken.

But that didn't stop Ted from joining with Hall of Fame defenceman Doug Harvey of the Montreal Canadiens and a small group of other players, and in 1957 they were successful in organizing the NHLPA. The group demanded a minimum salary and a properly funded pension plan. The best players in the league in those days earned around $25,000 a year, if you can imagine, and they didn't retire rich, as do many of today's players, even fourth-liners. Of course, the plans to get the players' association off the ground met with a backlash from the owners. Players suspected of being "union" sympathizers were banished to the minors, never to be heard from again. Lindsay was a star, so he was made an example of — Jack Adams traded him to Chicago along with Glenn Hall. Ultimately, in November of '57, Ted's former Red Wing teammates voted to withdraw from the players' association, and the organization collapsed. It would be another decade before the idea of an NHLPA took root.

Lindsay wasn't just a thug on the ice; he could play the game as well as any winger in history. As part of the famous Production Line with Gordie Howe and Sid Abel, Lindsay became one of the NHL's most dynamic players. In fact, in 1949–50, his sixth season in the NHL, Lindsay led the league in scoring and won the Art Ross Trophy with 23 goals and 78 points in 69 games. Detroit won the Stanley Cup that season, and won three more Cups while Lindsay wore the winged wheel.

There were some who played against Lindsay who wondered if he wasn't a little wacky. Once, at a game in Toronto, a death threat had been phoned in. A caller said that if Lindsay played in the game, he would be shot. Well, there was no intimidating Terrible Ted. He played, scored a goal, and after the game had ended, he stopped on his way back to the Detroit bench, turned his stick around as if it were a rifle and pointed it at the crowd, pretending to shoot.

Gordie Howe's reaction said it all: "I thought he was nuts."

Years later, I asked him, "Ted, why would you do something like that?"

"There's no reason," he said. "I just felt like making a point."

Ted simply had no fear. I think that's why he didn't get into a lot of fights — he was so unpredictable that guys would rather stay clear of him than get themselves into something they couldn't get out of … at least not with all their teeth and bones intact.

When Ted joined NBC as an analyst, I would play hockey with him on the NBC All-Stars against local college kids or NHL alumni teams, and the way he played, you'd think every shift was overtime in the seventh game of the Stanley Cup finals. The man was possessed! He'd give you shit if you missed a pass or made a wrong move. This was fun hockey? But that was Ted; he always wanted to win. I sure wouldn't want to play in another hockey game with him — never mind play against him. The funny thing is that afterwards he'd be calm and gentle.

Scotty Connal, our executive producer at NBC, signed him to be a colour commentator, even though he had no experience. And he did a great job. As director of the show, I made sure to spend a lot of time with Ted away from the arena so as to help my former boyhood idol look and sound as good as possible on the air. He was an eager student, and in the process I got to see a bit of his well-known competitive side as well as appreciate his intelligence.

Off the ice, Lindsay was one of the most elegant, cultured, self-educated men you would ever meet. He was a connoisseur of wine and food and a perfect gentleman with impeccable manners. He was also such a deep thinker. He wouldn't just spew opinions off the top of his head; instead, he would think things through before arriving at an opinion. Even today, Ted is never without an opinion on the game when asked, but his answers are well reasoned. Off the ice, there wasn't a better guy to go to the theatre or to dinner with. He was so cultured, you would think the guy was educated at Oxford, not St. Mike's. I always felt that what makes him such an interesting companion is that he is a great listener and loves to learn about new things. As Father David Bauer told me, "Ted is a deep person — very deep."

All of which meant that Ted became a damn good commentator. He took direction pretty well and was a fine partner for Tim Ryan, our play-by-play man. "When you are on camera," I'd tell him, "if Tim is speaking with you, look at Tim. Make it look just like two guys having a regular conversation." He said somebody had told him always to look at the camera, but I said that was nonsense — and, thankfully, he listened. He also accepted that he had to wear makeup — and that was a first.

Ted was on NBC for three years, and he got better with each game. He probably could have carved out a nice career for himself on television, but he was itching to get back into the game, and the next thing we knew, he was named general manager of the Red Wings. Imagine, the same guy who started the players' union and was unceremoniously traded away by the Red Wings is now the boss. Lindsay was okay as a general manager, but he never could have coached. He would have killed the players.

In 1978, *Hockey Night in Canada* was in Detroit for a playoff game against the Canadiens, and I was walking around the Olympia doing a survey. The Habs were practising on the ice, and their coach, Scotty Bowman, blew his whistle, calling the action to a halt. As usual, he was looking for an edge.

Bowman yelled to his players, "See? There's *Hockey Night in Canada* ... Mellanby. I want you guys to see this. *Hockey Night in Canada* is behind the Wings — there's Mellanby with Lindsay, and he's from Windsor."

I don't think there is anybody who can hold a grudge like Ted. But if you are a friend of Ted's then you are a friend for life. You're either with Ted or against him. Personally, I'm with him. Nobody could beat a team of Ted Lindsays. I am proud to have worked with him and consider it a distinct privilege to be called his friend.

Ted Lindsay is a survivor. He had trouble in a couple of business ventures, but always bounced back. He loves the game, but I don't think he loved the people in hockey. He hated Clarence Campbell — I know that for sure. When Ted came out of retirement in 1964–65 after four years away from the ice, Campbell said it was "a disgrace to hockey." Imagine Gary Bettman making such a public statement about a player today! By the way, Ted scored 14 goals and had 28 points that season, with 173 penalty minutes. Some disgrace! Indeed, Ted Lindsay is deserving of respect, and he was very deserving of being elected into the Hockey Hall of Fame in 1966. He had ferocity, he was fearless and he had courage.

Chapter 13

LARGER THAN LIFE
ROCKET RICHARD

["Gentlemen, take your hands off the greatest hockey player in the world." — Conn Smythe in the hallway at Toronto's Maple Leaf Gardens]

You grow up watching certain players, and then when you meet them they seem larger than life. Maurice "Rocket" Richard was one of those people. In Essex, Ontario, the Montreal Canadiens were our team and the Rocket was their best player.

Early in my television career in Windsor — I was a cameraman at the time — the Rocket was going to be a guest on a show that I was working on, hosted by Guy Nunn. I couldn't wait to meet him. In fact, the whole crew was hopping because the Rocket was in the building. Normally we had members of the Red Wings as our guests, but this was a rare treat: not only was a legendary Hab doing our program, but one who didn't like the limelight and wasn't big on making public appearances. It was quite a coup for our station. To be honest, I'm not really sure why he chose to do the show, but he was wonderful and gave a great interview.

The Rocket was in his prime, and when he walked into our building, it was as if a god was in our midst. When I got to meet him, I told him that a lot of guys around Windsor root for the Red Wings, but that back home in Essex I and most others rooted for him.

And why not? What wasn't to like?

The Rocket was one of the most ferocious and powerful players ever to skate in the NHL. It has been said that, from the blue line in, there was not a greater player in history, and I would agree. When the Rocket got the puck on his stick and drove to the net, nothing could stop him. The captain of the Canadiens from 1956–57 until he retired after the 1959–60 season, he won the Hart Trophy as the NHL's most valuable player in 1946–47, was a First Team All-Star eight times — including six years in a row — and a Second Team All-Star six times.

The one thing he never accomplished — and it's hard to believe — was to win the Art Ross Trophy as the league's top scorer. Of course, he was on the verge of winning it in 1955 when he was given a match penalty for deliberately injuring Boston's Hal Laycoe. During the melee that followed, Richard struck an official, the second time he had done so during the season, and he was suspended for the remainder of the year by the league's president, Clarence Campbell.

This suspension caused fans in Montreal to riot when Campbell attended the next Canadiens game at the Forum. When my pal Boom Boom Geoffrion passed the Rocket in the scoring race, Montreal fans even booed him.

While the Rocket didn't win a scoring title, he was the first player to score 50 goals in 50 games, and he retired as the NHL's all-time leading goal scorer with 544.

Dick Irvin used to tell me that not many people really got to know the Rocket because he was such a private man. And while *The Rocket*, the movie made about his life, portrays him as a political figure — indeed, a nationalist — I don't believe that to be the case. He was the most apolitical guy you could ever meet. He never got into politics, and his best friend, Ken Mosdell, was an English guy who didn't speak French.

I met him after he retired, when he was working with the Canadiens in the PR department. He would show up at functions and he was very conservative, very guarded. But those times that I spent with him, I found him to be very emotional.

On one occasion, a special night — a fundraiser — had been organized for me in Windsor, and there were all kinds of stars in attendance. Ronald Corey, who was president of the Montreal Canadiens, sent the Rocket to represent the team. I thought, "Wow! You can't do any better than the Rocket." Gordie Howe was there, too.

I'll never forget when the Rocket got on the stage with Dick Irvin. He got a ten-minute standing ovation. A lot of the people in the crowd were celebrities, so it just shows how strongly people felt about the Rocket, how much he was admired. On the night of the closing of the Montreal Forum, he got a twenty-minute standing ovation, and most of the people in attendance had never even seen him play.

After the fundraiser, we went to a party, and the Rocket sat among the other celebrities. He was very comfortable, since most of the people there were from the hockey world.

He said, "You know, Ralph, during that standing ovation tonight, I cried. I had to be careful nobody saw me. Why in Windsor? This is Red Wings country."

I told him, "Rocket, you would get this in Saskatoon. You would get this in Vancouver. People love you."

He thought he was revered only in Quebec. Of course, he was bigger than the Pope in Quebec! (René Lecavalier, our famous French broadcaster, used to tell the story that if a popularity vote were taken in Quebec, Richard would be the easy winner — because the Pope couldn't skate like the Rocket.)

It may have come as a surprise to Richard that night, but English Canada had a great appreciation not only for his talent and passion for the game, but also for what he meant to Quebec. I recall hearing that once, in the '40s, Richard was leaving the ice after an altercation and was jousting with the fans using his stick. Two Toronto policemen tried to step in, but Conn Smythe jumped out of the seats and said, "Gentlemen, take your hands off of the greatest hockey player in the world."

The Rocket proceeded to the dressing room, unharmed by the law.

The Rocket was fortunate, in a sense, to have hit it big during the television era. If he had retired earlier, around the time of players such as Howie Morenz and Milt Schmidt, I'm not certain people would have understood exactly how good a player he was. But people got to see him on television. They didn't have to take someone's word for it.

The Rocket retired in 1960 after having led Montreal to five straight Cups. I think he hung on for one year too long, but that being said, he still managed to score 19 goals and 35 points in 51 games. In the playoffs, though, he had just one goal in eight games. He was done.

But not completely. We had a *Hockey Night in Canada* all-star team that featured some pretty good players, including Bob Goldham and Brian McFarlane. We were playing a Montreal Canadiens old-timers team in Cornwall for charity one night, and some guy skated over to Brian and said, "Hey, you guys had better let the Rocket score."

Brian said, "Doesn't the Rocket always score? Why do we have to let him score?"

Of course he scored — on his own.

I knew the Rocket better away from the rink than I did as a player. He appeared on the *Don Cherry's Grapevine* show in Hamilton one year, and we had a limo pick him up at his hotel. He was a great guest, as usual, though I must say I felt a little uncomfortable when the talk turned to what is now called the Richard Riot.

I was fortunate to live ten years in Montreal, and even more lucky to be able to spend some time with Maurice Richard. He was always fun to sit and talk with and was always a gentleman. I appreciate what he meant to the people of Quebec.

Rocket was a shy but deeply religious man. And he just loved to play hockey. He and Gordie Howe shared two things in common — their passion for the game and the fact that they were as tough as nails. Nobody ever wanted to fight them. In those days, the best players were often also the best fighters.

As much of a competitor as the Rocket was, his teammates were always aware of another side of his personality. He was quite the practical joker. He would put soap or shaving cream in a guy's shoes, or put garbage in a guy's hat. He'd light a guy's newspaper on fire while he was reading it. Gilles Tremblay told me that you had to keep an eye on the Rocket.

The great Red Storey once told me that he and his fellow NHL referees also kept an eye on the Rocket — and looked out for him so that he could avoid trouble and suspensions. The late Terry Sawchuk, one of the greatest goalies ever, once said to me, "Of all the great players, Maurice was the one I feared the most. What people don't remember was how creative he could be with the puck. You just never knew what was going to happen when he skated in on you."

Chapter 14

THE GREATEST OF THEM ALL GORDIE HOWE

> ["Gordie Howe is the greatest of them all." — Lyrics from a 1960s song]

I count myself lucky because my television career enabled me to become friends of Gord and Colleen Howe. To have been in their company was always a great privilege and pleasure. To be around Gordie was to love him. He was hockey royalty, but also the easiest and best company you could ever keep — and, by the way, the funniest and cleverest hockey player I have ever known.

Gordie, or Mr. Hockey, as he became known, is the most distinctive individual I ever met in the National Hockey League. Start with the fact that he played twenty-five years with the Detroit Red Wings, retired for two years, then returned to play six seasons in the World Hockey Association alongside his sons, Marty and Mark — and then capped his career by playing one more season in the NHL at the age of fifty-one — and you have an idea of what I'm talking about.

Howe was an immensely gifted athlete who could easily have dominated any sport he played. Jack Adams, the longtime coach and general manager of the Detroit Red Wings, told me, "Gordie Howe could have been the heavyweight champion of the world … he could have been the best player in the National Football League … he could have been anything — the greatest athlete of his time."

Baseball Hall of Famer Al Kaline told me that Gordie, taking batting practice with the Detroit Tigers, drilled three balls out of the park to left field. Some of the Tigers, who were awestruck by his power, wondered, "Why aren't you playing baseball?"

Gordie just smiled and said, "I'm still trying to get it right playing hockey!"

At a charity all-star softball game I played in Amherstburg, Ontario, Gordie came up to the plate and did exactly what I thought he'd do: he smoked the ball over the fence. There were about 5,000 people in the stands and they went crazy.

What I admired most about Gordie was his humility. He was the greatest player in the NHL, yet his feet were planted firmly on the ground. As menacing as he could be on the ice, Gordie always made others feel comfortable and important. I'm not sure if Gordie knew exactly how big a star he was; if he did, he certainly didn't show it. He was always a regular guy from Saskatchewan and met most people with great ease.

Some of today's top athletes view their careers as limited windows of opportunity in which to earn as much as they can. And many become self-centred and standoffish. Not Gordie Howe. He was quite the opposite. When he was a superstar in the prime of his career in the mid-1950s, Gordie would drive over to the television station where I worked (CKLW in Windsor) to be interviewed — he even paid the tolls to drive through the Windsor–Detroit tunnel out of his own pocket! I can't imagine many of today's NHL players making such an effort. He'd arrive by himself — no such thing as an entourage — and by time he left, you'd think you had done him a favour by interviewing him.

I have known Gordie and Colleen Howe for more than fifty years and have shared many joyful experiences with them. And I've always loved Gordie's sense of humour.

Once, after a game between the Red Wings and the Canadiens, Gordie joined a group of people that included his agent, Gerry

Patterson, and baseball stars Gary Carter and Rusty Staub of the Montreal Expos. All were Patterson's clients at the time, and he wanted them to get to know one another. Rusty had a bit of an ego and had his girlfriend with him. I guess he was trying to impress her when he spoke about what a long-ball hitter he had been at a recent celebrity golf tournament.

Because of his huge forearms, Gordie always wore short-sleeved shirts. And, as he had just finished a game, he was hot. So he stood up and removed his jacket — and Staub's jaw dropped. He was dumbfounded. You had to see those shoulders, neck and arms to believe them.

"Yeah, I play in celebrity golf tournaments, too," Gordie said.

Colleen Howe piped up, "You know, Gordie can only take about three shots with each ball because he flattens them." She *wasn't* joking, as I well know. I've played with Howe, and he did wear out golf balls quickly.

Staub didn't say another word for the rest of the evening. He knew he was in the presence of Superman.

In the end, Gordie was known for his longevity — twenty-six years in the NHL and six more in the WHA. In his prime, though, he was regarded as the greatest combination of strength and skill the hockey world has ever seen. He could play the game any way you wanted it. You wanted to play a skill game? He'd outscore you. You wanted to get physical? He'd pummel you. In fact, because he could do it all — and often did in those days — any player who scores a goal, draws an assist and gets into a fight in a game is said to have completed a "Gordie Howe Hat Trick."

Born in Floral, Saskatchewan, in 1928, Gordie joined the Red Wings in 1946. He was a big farm boy whose strength and ultra-competitive nature quickly became legendary. It was almost as though there were two Gordie Howes — the kind and gentle soul who was aw-shucks shy off the ice, and the giant who would beat you senseless on it.

Gilles Tremblay, who played with the Montreal Canadiens — and who later worked for me on television — was often assigned to check

Howe, saw both sides of Mr. Hockey.

"You'd line up beside him at the faceoff and he'd say, 'Hello, Gilles. How's the wife? How's everything going?'" Tremblay recalled. "The next thing I know, I'm in the corner with him and my nose is broken. That's Gordie Howe for you."

Gordie and I met in the '50s, but our relationship grew after I began working with *Hockey Night in Canada*. Once, while we were at an NHL All-Star Game, Gordie spied me standing in the lobby of the Queen Elizabeth Hotel in Toronto.

"Ralph," he bellowed, "what are you doing?"

"Waiting for my new wife, Janet." Janet had never met Gordie or Colleen Howe.

He said, "Hey, let's have lunch. Colleen is here. The four of us should eat together. Two greats from Saskatchewan [he had heard Janet was born there] should get to know one another."

There's Gordie's humour for you. And Janet and Colleen became good friends.

Gordie was always looking to make people laugh. Once, in the '60s, after playing in a celebrity golf tournament, we were both naked in the locker room when Gordie turned and said to me, "Don't ever lose your tailor, Ralphie."

Another time, when we played in the first NHL golf tournament in Vermont, Gordie duffed his first tee shot.

"I knew I was going to have a good game," he said. "Can I have a Ralph Mulliganby?"

Then he proceeded to hit the ball 300 yards.

If Gordie poked fun at anyone, though, it was mainly himself.

At the All-Star Game in St. Louis in 1970, we interviewed Gordie between periods. I was in the corner studio with Dave Hodge, who did the interview, and when we finished, Gordie plopped himself down into a chair.

I said, "We're done ... you can go, Gordie."

"No way, Ralph," he replied. "I'm staying put here."

"Why?"

It turned out that Gordie had a little tear in the shoulder area of his jersey and he didn't want the all-star coach, Claude Ruel of the Canadiens, to see it.

"That guy drives me nuts," Gordie said. "His pre-game instruction to the team was to stay up, stay up, come back, come back and don't hurt the new all-star sweaters! Look at my sweater."

Gordie sat there until the rest of the players skated onto the ice, and he then joined his teammates.

There have been bigger, faster, stronger, more skilled players in the NHL, but none possessed the combination of all those attributes that Number 9 did. By the time he retired for good in 1980, after playing one last NHL season with the Hartford Whalers, Howe had amassed 801 goals and 1,850 points in 1,767 NHL games. To those totals, add another 174 goals and 508 points in 419 games in the WHA. He led the NHL in scoring six times, was awarded the Hart Trophy as the NHL's most valuable player six times and helped Detroit win four Stanley Cups. Amazing!

When *The Hockey News* compiled a list of the top 100 players of all time, Howe ranked third behind Wayne Gretzky and Bobby Orr.

Although he was called Big Gordie, he only stood six feet tall and weighed 200 pounds — that would make him slightly smaller than average in today's league. Gord wasn't the type of player to go looking for a fight, but when he was challenged, look out! When Gordie first joined the NHL, there was a player with the Rangers who used to chop away at his ankles. Gordie was annoyed and finally said to the guy, "If you keep doing that, I'm going to knock your head off."

Well, the next time Detroit played the Rangers, this guy was chopping away at Gordie's ankles. So Gordie hauled off and clobbered him. Then, as the Ranger lay flat on the ice, Gordie leaned over him and said, "I didn't knock your head off, but I sure as hell loosened it." Another example of the Howe humour.

On February 1, 1959, Rangers tough-guy Lou Fontinato found out exactly how menacing Howe could be. In Gordie's first fight in nine years, he beat Fontinato to a pulp, breaking his nose and leaving him a bloody mess.

"I'm going to tell you a secret," Gordie once told me. "I saw him charging at me in the reflection in the glass. I turned and timed it perfectly. Nailed him right in the jaw — end of fight!"

Gordie should have been a Red Wing for life. Then again, if he had played for Detroit his entire career, he never would have earned what he was worth. Even though he was the NHL's best player, he was treated like just another player. He was loyal to a fault to the Red Wings, and because of that they never paid him what he was worth. Year in and year out, Gordie would just keep signing whatever contract Jack Adams put in front of him. The Wings took him for granted.

That changed after Bobby Baun was traded from the Oakland Seals to the Red Wings. He and Gordie went out for lunch, and Baun set him straight. "What's wrong with you? You're the biggest star in the NHL and I'm making $20,000 a year more than you."

Howe was shocked.

Ultimately, Colleen Howe took over the job of managing Gordie's career. It was Colleen and agent Gerry Patterson who put together the deal to have Gordie play with Marty and Mark in the WHA. Some people resented Colleen, because in that era it wasn't customary for a player's wife to be involved in his career. But I admired her. Colleen used to phone and consult me when Gordie was offered television appearances to see if he was getting a good deal. I felt honoured that she valued my opinion, though I later found out she did the same thing with others in the industry. She would gather as much information as she could before making her final decision. Smart gal!

I was extremely sad when Colleen became ill with Pick's disease. It made for a sad final chapter in the life of a very vibrant and beautiful woman. Gordie and Colleen Howe are one of the greatest love stories of all time. They were the perfect linemates — the perfect partners.

We used Gordie a few times as an analyst on *Hockey Night* and on networks in the States, and he was good. The only problem was that, being the good-natured man he was, Gordie would never say a bad word about anybody. It's not as though we encouraged our guys to rip people, but the reality is, when you are analyzing a game, you need to be prepared to point out mistakes. You have to call 'em as you see 'em. And when you do that, at the end of the day there's a very good chance somebody is going to be pissed off with you. Gordie didn't like that. When I joined NBC for their *Game of the Week* broadcasts, I was asked about hiring Gordie and told them the same thing — it just wasn't his cup of tea.

"He is a great hockey ambassador, not a great colour man," I said.

Our sons played together with the Philadelphia Flyers. Mark Howe and Scott became close, which gave the Howes and the Mellanbys a great deal of joy — and gave Gordie more material. "Our kids are great players!" he would say. "I knew Scott had great hockey bloodlines ... too bad about Mark."

Of course, Mark Howe had the pedigree, but I'm not sure where Scott got his talent. Let's just say hockey was not my game — baseball, perhaps, but not hockey!

When I speak about hockey forwards, I say that from the blue line in there was nobody greater than Rocket Richard. The most talented player offensively was Wayne Gretzky. But the most complete, without a doubt, was Number 9, Gordie Howe.

Chapter 15

THE DIAMOND IN THE ROUGH BOBBY HULL

Nobody in the history of the NHL treated the fans as well as Bobby Hull did. He was famous for holding up the team bus long after games had ended to sign autographs for anybody and everybody who approached him. He treated his parents and his brothers like gold, too. I recall once, in Montreal, he had his mom and dad right down at ice level with him as he signed autographs. I'll never forget the look of pride on his parents' faces. He took his mom and dad everywhere with him. There are a lot of stories about Bobby, about how he acted away from the rink, but any guy who treats his parents like Bobby treated his must be admired.

Once, for *Hockey Night in Canada*, we filmed a feature on Bobby in Toronto, following him from the Royal York Hotel onto the subway — can you believe players went to Maple Leaf Gardens by subway back then? — and then during the walk to the players' entrance of the arena. He signed autographs the whole way, and what should have been a twenty-minute trip wound up taking two hours.

On the ice, he was one of the greatest combinations of power and grace the NHL has ever seen. He and Stan Mikita perfected the curved stick, and man, could he ever shoot the puck. Goalies trembled at the mere thought of getting in the way of a Bobby Hull slapshot. Hull's shot was clocked at well over 100 miles per hour. And to think, goalies didn't wear masks for much of Hull's career.

Although he stood only five foot ten, Hull was as muscular as a

Greek god. In fact, one of the most famous pictures of Hull from his glory days is of him on the back of a wagon in the off-season, shirtless, pitching hay, with muscles that made him look like Arnold Schwarzenegger.

Hull joined the Chicago Black Hawks in 1957–58, the same year that Frank Mahovlich, who was named the NHL's rookie of the year (Hull was runner-up), broke in with the Toronto Maple Leafs. While Mahovlich would go on to have a Hall of Fame career and become one of the best left wingers ever, Hull developed into a bona fide superstar and *the* best left winger of all time. Three times he won the Art Ross Trophy as the NHL's top scorer (1960, 1962 and 1966), and twice he was awarded the Hart Trophy as the NHL's most valuable player (1965 and 1966). He was a First Team All-Star ten times, a Second Team All-Star twice, and ranked eighth on *The Hockey News*'s list of the 100 greatest hockey players. Naturally, he was the top-ranked left winger.

I remember one time when he first joined the NHL, the Black Hawks (the team's nickname was two words until 1986–87, when it became Blackhawks) were in Detroit and the score was about 5–0 late in the game when my younger brother, Jim, asked me if we should hop in the car and head home.

"No way!" I said. I wanted to stay and watch Hull play one more shift. I was twenty-three at the time and had never seen anything so beautiful as Bobby Hull's skating. He was the greatest player I had ever seen; there's no way I was passing on the opportunity to see him skate every shift I could in person. I had never seen anybody skate like Hull in my life.

I had seen Howie Morenz on film, and when I asked Hall of Famer Newsy Lalonde about him, he said Morenz was "exactly like Bobby Hull. They both had such grace. When you watch Hull, you are seeing Howie Morenz."

Hull was an explosive player, but he was always surrounded by a lot of controversy. He had a well-earned reputation for being a playboy and was once accused, by his first wife, Joanne, of assaulting her. Theirs was a tumultuous relationship, to say the least. Once, after Bobby had been out the night before, Joanne stood angrily behind the glass, scowling at her husband as the Hawks took their pre-game warm-up. Bobby told me he fired a slapshot that hit the glass in front of her. It's lucky, with his powerful shot, that the glass didn't shatter.

"Maybe I should shoot at her," Stan Mikita suggested. "I have a harder shot than you do."

"Be my guest," Bobby replied.

The stories about Hull off the ice are legendary. The fact is, Stan was no choirboy, either. The Chicago organization knew what it had in its two biggest stars, and I think it protected them both. We all knew Hull's personal life was nothing to rave about, but the press guarded him.

After fifteen years with Chicago, Hull shocked the hockey world by jumping to the fledgling World Hockey Association. The Winnipeg Jets gave him a $1 million contract — an unheard-of sum of money at the time — and he gave the WHA instant credibility. He also helped drive up salaries in the NHL: his decision to play in the WHA caused NHL owners to pony up more money to keep stars who were threatening to jump to the rival league. He ultimately returned to the NHL, playing for Winnipeg and Hartford in 1979–80, but he was only a shadow of the star he had been. Like so many other great athletes, he hung on too long.

Hull retired with 610 goals and 1,170 points in 1,063 NHL games, plus another 303 goals and 638 points in 411 WHA games. Amazing numbers!

It was as a player in the WHA that Hull first displayed a political side. Sick and tired of all the fighting that was taking place in hockey, Hull staged a one-game protest against hockey violence in 1977–78. Hull was so strong that he probably could have pummelled three-quarters of the players he played against, if not more, but the older he grew, the less tolerant he was of what he considered a senseless form of intimidation and a sideshow in an otherwise great sport. Though fighting is still a part of hockey today, it has been reduced to what NHL officials have called a reasonable level, and there are rarely bench-clearing brawls, a staple of '70s hockey.

It wasn't the last time Bobby would be heard from in a political vein.

* * *

Bobby had such charm that I thought he would be a natural on television. And he was ... for a while. When he was a player, nobody could be more accommodating than Hull. We did more stuff with him than any other player. He was great to work with; he seemed to understand the importance of star players selling the sport and never had to be coaxed into helping us out.

Bobby was fun to be with — a pleasure to have dinner with — and to watch him interact with people was a real experience. What charisma! I got to know him well when I was at CBS, and the experience over a few weeks was good. Bobby worked with Dan Kelly one year during the playoffs, and he worked hard, going to practices to gather information. He had such a great smile, and the only minus was that he was often distracted by his hair. He was always checking it out — he couldn't stand the fact that he was going bald.

When he was with CBS, you couldn't have asked for a greater guy. He was at the top of his game. His work with *Hockey Night in Canada* was a different story. He only ended up lasting a year with us.

It was just after Hull had retired from the Hartford Whalers. Maybe I was thinking back to that awesome player I'd seen at the Olympia in Detroit. Maybe my dream was to make Bobby a television superstar. I don't know.

Frank Selke, who was one guy I truly respected, and who had rejoined *HNiC* after he was finished as general manager in Oakland, suggested that having Bobby Hull on the broadcast would be a mistake. "Ralph," he said, "you're breaking your own rule." He was referring to the fact that, for me, character and conduct were the most important prerequisites for anyone joining the *Hockey Night in Canada* team.

I respected his judgment, but I stuck my neck out for Hull and hired him anyway. Looking back, I should have listened to Frank.

I met with Bobby in Montreal, and our meeting went well. He felt that being on *Hockey Night in Canada* would be great. He said — with a chuckle, I might add — "It'll give me something to do on the weekend."

I suggested to Bobby that we sit down and I would teach him how we do things the *Hockey Night in Canada* way. "We don't have to do that," he replied.

I should have known right away that this was going to be difficult.

I said I'd team him with Dick Irvin, whom I respected greatly. Hull would be the third man in the booth with Irvin and Danny Gallivan. Bobby thought that would be great. I had an ulterior motive in making this choice: I figured Dick could teach Bobby to prepare for the broadcasts, because nobody prepared himself better for a broadcast than Dick Irvin. In fact, I used to pair every colour man or analyst I hired with Dick at first, to give them a running start. Guys such as Gary Dornhoefer and Mickey Redmond benefited greatly from Irvin's tutelage. Put them with him for just one day and the results were amazing.

I liked Hull's performance in his first broadcast, and when it concluded, I said to Dick, "Bobby was pretty good."

"Ralph," Irvin replied, "all he had was a program — no notes, no preparation. He just ad libs."

We used him every three or four weeks, and he remained very good on camera. But he never bothered to prepare; he'd just react to what he saw and what was being said. And he was very candid. For instance, someone might ask, "So, Bobby, what do you think of the new offside rule?"

"I think it stinks!"

Sounds a lot like Brett Hull, his superstar son who works in television now after a glorious NHL career of his own. Must be in the genes.

I thought Bobby was coming along nicely, but every time I used him as the third man in the booth, the reports I got back confirmed that he would just show up with a program. He wasn't working at the job.

Bobby would say to me, "Ralph, I don't like walking around with a lot of paper. I memorize things. I keep it all up here in my ass!"

I liked Bobby on camera; my mistake was in putting him in the booth. I should have assigned him to work during the intermissions with Dave Hodge instead. There, he could have commented on each period for a few minutes instead of having to have things to say throughout the game.

In early 1984, I left to do the Winter Olympics in Sarajevo. While I was there, I picked up the paper and read that Hull had taken all of his stuff out of the Hockey Hall of Fame. Here was a guy who I thought was coming along nicely for us on *HNiC*, one of the great superstars of hockey, and suddenly out of left field (at least to me) he was in a battle with the NHL.

I got a call from my boss, Ted Hough, and another from league president John Ziegler, telling me we couldn't have Bobby Hull on the show anymore.

"I am not firing Bobby Hull," I insisted. "If he has problems with the NHL, it has nothing to do with us. We don't have problems with him."

There I was, still thinking Hull was a guy I could mould into a pretty good broadcaster. I suggested we have Bobby on the show and let him tell his side, then have someone from the NHL on and allow them to speak their piece. Besides, I figured the publicity would help us. If people knew Bobby was going to be on and speaking about his disagreement with the league, it would drive our ratings through the ceiling.

Immediately I got on the phone with Bobby.

"What are you doing?" I asked him.

He said, "I am resigning from the Hall of Fame and I am quitting *HNiC*."

Here I was, going to bat for him and putting my own job on the line, and now he was up and quitting? This was like some kind of bad dream.

"You can't quit," I said. "Let us give you a chance to tell your side of the story on the show."

He said, "No. I quit," and hung up on me. I tried to get back in touch with him, to no avail.

I guess he thought *HNiC* was an arm of the NHL. That may have been true once, but it certainly was no longer the case. I stood up for Bobby Hull, just like I stood up for my guys in the past and would in the future. But he wanted no part of it.

I got back to Toronto after the Olympics, by which time Bobby hadn't been on for a few weeks. Dave Hodge finally made an announcement on *Hockey Night.*

"You have probably noticed Bobby Hull hasn't been on in a while," Hodge said. "We wanted Bobby to stay with the show, but regrettably, he has resigned."

I never got a formal resignation from him, nor did I hear from his agent. He had a contract, but it was never fulfilled. It all just faded away.

That summer I called Bobby to see if he would be a guest on the "Hockey Legends" show with Bobby Orr. He may have quit on me, but that didn't make him any less of a legend.

He said, "You have the nerve to call me and ask me to be on your show?"

So I got Orr to call him. Hull wouldn't appear on the show for me, but he would for Orr. I often wonder how the 1972 Summit Series would have turned out if Team Canada had had those two guys. Both were in the prime of their careers, but Orr's knee was too sore for him to play, and the NHL wouldn't allow Hull to play because he had jumped to the WHA.

When Hull got to Jamaica, he was fine. He accepted the direction I gave him and, in fact, was very nice … very affable. Typically, he was gracious to my family. And every time I have seen Bobby Hull since, he has been great with me.

"Hey, Ralph, how ya doing?" he'd say. He never mentions the *Hockey Night in Canada* incident — never!

I still really don't understand what happened. But I do know I was ready to fight for him. I had made a commitment to him, and I thought he had made one to me. I don't think he should have quit. He should have come on the air and told his side of the story and continued to do the show.

One thing about Bobby is that he just never seemed to understand when to turn it off, to tone things down, particularly in mixed company. I think Bobby Orr once put it best when we were doing the "Hockey Legends" series. Hull showed up, and I had my wife and kids — who were then in their early teens — with me. Anyway, we were sitting at the dinner table and Hull started telling off-colour jokes.

Orr would tell most people to knock it off, but he just looked at me and shrugged. "Diamond in the rough, Ralph. Diamond in the rough."

The next day, Hull took my twelve-year-old son, Scott, deep-sea fishing. I was a little afraid to let Scott go, because I was filming that day and wouldn't be able to join them. I told Bobby of my concern, but he just winked at me and said, "Don't worry, Ralph. I'll keep an eye on him."

I have never been as confused about an individual as I was about Bobby Hull.

I think he could have had a decent television career, but it wasn't to be. Later, he worked some Ontario Hockey League junior games, but that didn't last too long either.

I liked Bobby Hull, but for some reason he wanted to distance himself from the NHL forever. And he saw *HNiC* as part of the problem.

Orr was dead right: Bobby Hull is indeed a diamond in the rough. And what a great hockey player he was, too — a real gem of a guy.

Chapter 16

ONE OF A KIND
BOBBY ORR

If I had to find words to describe Bobby Orr, they would be "talented" and "complex" — yes, very complex.

He was, without question, the greatest defenceman ever to play in the National Hockey League, a superb athlete who dominated and revolutionized the sport like no other. Orr was a gifted skater, puck handler and scorer who had the uncanny ability to control the pace of a game.

There are many who claim Orr is the greatest player of all time; I have too much respect and admiration for Wayne Gretzky, and the mark he left on the sport, to make that distinction. Suffice it to say, though, that if I were starting an NHL team, I would be delighted to have either of them playing for me.

Orr's career was cut short by injuries, and his business relationship with his agent and trusted adviser, Alan Eagleson, had failed. Which meant that, by the time I became his producer and partner in "Hockey Legends," the native of Parry Sound, Ontario, had become reclusive, withdrawn and very suspicious of nearly everybody he dealt with. While I enjoyed a very fruitful and close working relationship with Orr after his playing days, I am not sure I knew the real Bobby Orr.

I first heard all about the teenage phenom who was taking the hockey world by storm from an old friend of mine, Wren Blair. At fourteen years old, Orr was a member of the Oshawa Generals of the Ontario Hockey Association, playing against young men five and six years older — and revolutionizing the way the game was played. He was a one-man wrecking crew, able to beat you on the scoreboard, yet tough enough to beat you in the alley. The NHL — particularly the Boston Bruins, who owned his rights — were licking their chops, just waiting until the day he turned pro.

It's not as though Orr was the first defenceman to make a significant contribution in terms of offence; the great Eddie Shore of the Boston Bruins created a template for offensive-minded blueliners in the 1920s and '30s, and Doug Harvey was as fine a playmaker as you'd ever find throughout his illustrious eighteen-year NHL career, most of it with the Montreal Canadiens.

Orr was different. He didn't just chip in on offence; he ran the show. He could take the puck behind his team's net and tear up the ice with his legs spread wide to prevent checkers from knocking him over, and he wouldn't dispose of the puck until he chose to. His ability to pass to the open man was unparalleled, and his shot was one of the best in all of hockey. He was the first defenceman to lead the NHL in scoring, in 1970 and again in 1975, and he won the James Norris Trophy as the NHL's best defenceman eight years in a row.

I was there when Bobby made his NHL debut at Boston Garden in 1966. It was my first year as executive producer of *Hockey Night in Canada*, and we were broadcasting the game on CBC Radio. Because it was a special night, the decision was made to carry the game coast to coast. The Toronto Maple Leafs — our number one attraction across Canada — had the night off, so Orr had the stage all to himself, playing against the Detroit Red Wings.

I had seen great hockey games, as well as amazing players, in my life, but this was a night that stood head and shoulders above the others. There was an electric charge in the building as Bruins fans who had waited patiently for the arrival of this wonder kid finally got the opportunity to see him up close. The Bruins had been mediocre for so long, missing the playoffs in each of the previous seven seasons, that Orr's arrival was seen as the harbinger of a rebirth of the franchise. When he skated onto the ice for the pre-game warm-up, the capacity crowd quickly rose to their feet and gave him a standing ovation. He hadn't done a thing yet, but the Bruins fans clapped enthusiastically and chanted his name. Danny Gallivan said he had never seen an audience react this way to any player before.

Orr scored a goal that night, but otherwise didn't do anything spectacular; still, we knew that we had witnessed the arrival of a player who would dominate the sport, even if we still had no idea exactly how good this young man would turn out to be. I loved Bobby Orr from that first day I saw him at the Boston Garden. I figured he was going to be the greatest thing for hockey.

Looking back, I am amazed that we didn't interview Orr during our broadcast. Times have changed. Today, when a potential young superstar arrives in the NHL, the media is all over him. Consider the attention paid to Gretzky, or to Eric Lindros or Sidney Crosby.

The next time I met Orr, we were televising a game in Montreal. My television room was situated between the French and English studios, across from the visitors' dressing room. In the back, we had a lounge, so that if a player came in to be interviewed he could sit down while he waited to go on the air. We weren't about to let Bobby get away this time without being part of our broadcast.

It was Saturday night, and my wife, Janet, was with me in the room at the time. She would often join me at the games, and would watch the proceedings as I went about my business. My runner brought an exhausted Bobby Orr into the room for his interview and gave him the usual drink and a towel. As Janet got up to give Bobby her seat, Bobby refused, saying, "No, ma'am, you sit, please."

Ninety percent of players would have allowed her to get up and would have taken the seat, forcing Janet to move. Not Bobby, though. He was polite and considerate. Both Janet and I were suitably impressed with this young gentleman. I'll never forget how graciously he treated Janet. He was a superstar and always acted like one.

That evening, I introduced myself to Bobby. It was to be the beginning of a long-lasting relationship.

For me, one of the qualities that stood out the most was his humility. He could do things on the ice that other players only dreamed of, yet he never seemed to place himself above others. There were no goofy celebrations after scoring a goal or hot-dogging for the cameras; just a young man who used his unnatural ability to help his team the best he could, with no sense of being entitled to praise or a reward.

Players used to tell me that Orr would do things in practice that nobody else could do — things like a triple reverse, or dragging the puck and putting it between his legs. But he would never do these things in games. Phil Esposito told me it was because Orr was unselfish and never wanted to embarrass the opposition. "You know," Phil would say, "if I could do those things, I'd do them in games." But not Bobby. He was just that humble.

I have always wondered, as has Don Cherry, what plays we might have witnessed if Bobby had not respected his opponents so much, if he had been more of a showman. I remember directing a Bruins game for NBC in which Bobby took the puck and circled the net with an opponent in hot pursuit. To shake the checker, Bobby skated around his own net three times before finally dashing up the ice. As he raced into the other team's zone, he faked a pass and, with the goalie charging out at him, circled the opposition's net and quietly slid the puck into the yawning cage. What I remember most about this spectacular play was the shot that a cameraman captured of him gliding back to the bench. Bobby was hunched over, almost embarrassed by the clinic he had put on —and what he had just put the other team through. He didn't like showing up opponents, but at the same time he had skill that simply could not be contained.

This was just a glimpse of what Bobby was capable of. But in his prime, he always held back.

I finally got to know Bobby on more of a business level after his career ended. When you're not a player, you're not really in their clique. Obviously, I had never been a player, nor had I managed a team, so there really wasn't any chance for Bobby and me to forge a relationship while he was still playing. Because Alan Eagleson and

I were close, however, our paths would cross once in a while.

One of Orr's closest friends, even to this day, was his coach, Don Cherry. Don knew a good thing when he saw one and quickly established two sets of rules for the Bruins: one for Bobby and one for the rest of the team. Even though he has become a celebrity in his own right, Don still fawns over Orr like an adoring father would a successful son.

We televised Bobby Orr Night — the night the Bruins celebrated his retirement. Cherry was absolutely disgusted by the fact that Orr was being honoured on the night of an exhibition game — and against the Russians, of all teams. "Unacceptable," Don said. In protest, he flatly refused to dress his star players. How could these people insult Bobby Orr?

I remember that Harry Sinden was furious.

Bobby told me about one time when Cherry was really unhappy with the way the team was playing. He ordered the defencemen to stay on the ice after practice for a stern lecture.

"When you get the puck, move it — pass it!" Cherry barked. "If I have to tell you again, I'll sit your ass down or I'll send you down to the minors!"

Chastened, the defencemen headed to the dressing room. Cherry called Bobby back.

"Bobby," he said, "you do whatever the hell you want."

As the producer of *Hockey Night in Canada*, I used to show up early for games, particularly in the playoffs. If the game were at 7 p.m., I'd be at the rink by 10 a.m. to supervise. It never ceased to amaze me that, no matter what time I arrived at the rink, Bobby would already be in the Bruins' dressing room. They would have their morning skate, then head back to the hotel for a meal and a nap, but Bobby would stay at the rink all day. He just couldn't wait to play the game. I'm certain that if he could have, Bobby would have lived at the rink. You could feel his love for the game. He was a heart and soul hockey player.

My biggest regret concerning Bobby is that we never saw how

great he could have been on two good legs. He injured his knee early in his career and it hampered his ability to play for the rest of his days. He won the Norris Trophy so often it should be called the Orr Trophy, but I still don't think we really saw how dominant he could have been.

It's also a crime that Bobby never played the Russians in his prime. He faced them in the Canada Cup in 1976 and was great, being named the tournament's most valuable player, but he was nowhere near as dominant as he could have been had he been 100 percent healthy. In his prime, Bobby would have eaten the Russians alive. They were great athletes and fabulous players, but they had never faced the likes of Bobby Orr. If they put three men on him, he would have beaten all three and led Canada on a four-on-two rush up the ice.

In my opinion, if Bobby had been available to play in the famous 1972 Summit Series, it would have been a different series, especially on the big ice in Russia. Would Paul Henderson, who scored the game-winning goals in each of the final three games, have been the hero? Who knows?

Team Canada didn't have the great Bobby Hull, either. He snubbed the NHL by signing with the fledgling World Hockey Association and was not invited.

With the two Bobbys in the lineup, I have no doubt that the '72 series would not have been as close as it wound up being. Those two players would have made a huge difference.

* * *

After Bobby split with Eagleson in a bitter dispute over Orr's finances, Bill Watters took over his career. At this time, even the great Bobby Orr suffered from the malaise of all retirees: lack of exposure. I met with Watters, and we agreed that Bobby needed to revitalize his career. He needed a platform. Bobby wasn't going to be a full-time analyst — I tried him on several occasions and he was great, but it wasn't something he wanted.

So I came up with "Bobby Orr and the Hockey Legends," a filmed series featuring Bobby with some of the game's brightest stars. The episodes would be shot each summer at a resort in Jamaica. It was something I had always wanted to do because I love the heritage of the game and wanted it to be highlighted on *Hockey Night in Canada*.

I was to produce the shows, and Watters, who loved the idea, sold Bobby on the concept. Right away, I got an idea of what it was going to be like to deal with Bobby Orr. After his split with Eagleson, he would never again allow anybody to lead him down the garden path. The sponsor would be Standard Brands — Bobby's main sponsor. We met at the Four Seasons Hotel in Toronto, and it immediately became apparent that this was not going to be the Ralph Mellanby Show ... it was going to be the Bobby Orr Show. Bobby made it absolutely clear that he wanted a say in the production, which was fine by me.

Without question, Bobby Orr is the most inquisitive athlete I have ever encountered. He wanted to know everything about the production — not only how things were done, but why. He was an absolute perfectionist. No matter what it took to get things right, Bobby was willing to do it. If it required ten takes to get the shot he wanted, Bobby would do ten takes. Above all, he always seemed to be suspicious about everything — the writer, the crew, the locations — and I had to alleviate those suspicions. Which I did, and I never asked why.

I was the director, but Bobby was really the producer. He had so much input on pretty much every aspect of the show. It surprised me a bit. I'm not exactly certain what I expected, but I know I was shocked at how hands-on he was. Here's a guy who was a hockey player, but he wanted to learn the filming business — the television business — and he wanted to make sure nothing got by him.

I am now certain that this had a lot to do with what had happened between him and Eagleson. He looked back and realized that he hadn't asked enough questions about what was going on, and he wasn't about to repeat that mistake. (By the way, we had an agreement never to talk about Eagleson, who was still my friend.)

We got along fabulously. We did the show for six years on *Hockey Night*, and it was well received.

Bobby had his regimen and his own way of doing the job. He met the guest the day before shooting, and we would always have to eat at a place where Bobby would not be bothered — in a private room. Some might think that was a little strange, but who was I to question this great young man? Bobby had to have things his way, and I wasn't against that. Bobby was a superstar; I was his support. It worked.

Hollywood legend Orson Welles, with whom I had dinner one evening at the Boulevard Club in Toronto, once told me that the greatest thing you can do for performers and actors is to make them feel comfortable and secure. I remembered that advice and applied it to Bobby.

One guest we disagreed over was Don Cherry. Bobby wanted him, while I didn't.

You have to remember that Cherry only had one year on *HNiC* under his belt at that time, and I knew he wasn't there yet. I was building him into a television personality and didn't want to do anything to mess up Don Cherry or embarrass him. Today, I would easily say, "Of course … he should be our pilot show." In 2004, viewers of a CBC Television series would vote him the seventh-greatest Canadian. But back then, Don Cherry was not the Don Cherry we all know today. He was developing. Even Cherry felt that he wasn't a "hockey legend." It was strictly because he was Bobby's pal that he was going to be a part of the show.

Bobby and I had an argument on the phone. I told him, "Don Cherry is not a legend … maybe someday he will be, but he's not one now. He played one game in the NHL, never won the Stanley Cup … how do you think he's a legend?"

"Well, *I* think he's a legend," Orr insisted.

I said, "I will not do Don Cherry."

"Then you won't be the director," was Bobby's reply. It proved to be the breaking point in our relationship on the show. I brought in another director for the series.

We got back together — don't get me wrong — but our relationship working on "Hockey Legends" was never the same. I continued to be involved in the show behind the scenes, but I let somebody else direct.

Bobby never apologized for his stance, and I certainly didn't apologize for mine. It was a disagreement; that's all. He's a professional and so was I.

I must say today that Bobby was right. It was our best show.

Bobby worked for me at the 1979 Challenge Cup, providing analysis. I felt he did a very good job, and it was a bonus to have him be a part of any broadcast. I liked him as the third man in the booth, always with Dick Irvin, but he accepted my invitation only a few times.

* * *

One of my fondest memories of Bobby Orr came during the 1974 Stanley Cup finals, when the Bruins were facing the Philadelphia Flyers. Back in 1969, the Flyers had adopted Kate Smith's rendition of "God Bless America" as their anthem; rather than playing "The Star-Spangled Banner" before home games, they would often play a recording of Smith belting out the patriotic tune. Over the years, it had become a good luck charm for the Flyers, who posted a record of 64 wins, 15 losses and 3 ties in games begun with "God Bless America."

Game 6 of the series, to be played at the Spectrum in Philadelphia, found the Flyers leading three games to two, setting up the possibility that they might win the Stanley Cup on home ice. For only the second time in team history, arrangements had been made for Smith to travel to Philadelphia to sing "God Bless America" in person. Management kept things tightly under wraps — no one, not even the players, had been told of Smith's surprise appearance. The team had to tell me, of course, because I was producing the broadcast of the game, and I had to plan for the production. They told me her musical accompaniment would be on tape, but Kate's vocal would be live. And I was instructed to keep it under my hat.

I knew the crowd would go nuts and it would make for great television. At the same time, I wondered if the performance might give the Flyers an unfair advantage. I wanted the Bruins to be prepared for what was about to take place. They needed an equal chance to respond.

After the morning skate, I took Bobby and Phil Esposito aside and said, "I want to let you in on a little something that is going to happen tonight. Now, I trust you guys so keep this to yourselves, but be prepared."

I told them Kate Smith was going to make a surprise live appearance.

"Kate Smith? I didn't even know she was alive," Phil said. "Is she alive?"

They went out and got her a huge bouquet of flowers — I'm certain it was Bobby's idea. Bobby and Phil presented the flowers after the anthem, and that apparently negated the advantage the Flyers might have gained. It also lent a classy finish to a great moment.

Mind you, the Flyers won the Cup that night, so in hindsight, maybe it really didn't matter.

* * *

Over the years, Orr and I worked on television and golfed and played tennis together. In tennis, he hated when I would lob the ball over his head, because he would have to chase it down with his gimpy knee — always the competitor. When he was inducted into the Hockey Hall of Fame and Canada's Sports Hall of Fame, he invited me to the ceremonies. I also attended the Bobby Orr Hall of Fame ceremonies in Parry Sound.

It gives me great pleasure that my son, Scott, sees Robert — which is what I always called Bobby — from time to time and has played golf with him at some NHL functions.

Bobby Orr is classy, bright, talented and inquisitive. But I'm sorry to say that he is also one of the most wounded and suspicious athletes I have ever known. The bottom line, however, is that I am proud to have known him and to have worked beside him.

Chapter 17

THE ARTIST FRANK MAHOVLICH

> "Don't ever wake him up or you will pay the price. For then you will see the greatest hockey player that ever lived." — John Ferguson on why he never fought or bothered the Big M

I don't think Frank Mahovlich ever comprehended exactly how good a hockey player he was — or how much better he could have been.

I remember once, when I was watching a Toronto–Montreal playoff game, Frank took the puck in his team's zone and began skating. Frank, unquestionably one of the most powerful, yet graceful, skaters in history, approached Montreal defenceman Terry Harper, who was a friend of mine. Rather than go around Harper, Mahovlich steamrolled him — ran right over him. *Kaboom!* Now, Terry Harper was a big guy — and he was out cold.

The funny thing is, I don't think Frank ever realized what he did. He just went about his business, because that was what Frank Mahovlich did.

Frank seemed to live in his own world. To describe him would be difficult, because he was such a unique guy. His younger brother, Peter, who enjoyed a fruitful professional career of his own, was a charismatic, happy-go-lucky guy who loved life and wasn't afraid to show it. Frank, on the other hand, was sensitive and often moody. He was definitely tightly wound and unpredictable.

I knew Frank well when he played in the NHL, and he was my favourite player. I loved his style and enjoyed just watching him skate. When he retired after a splendid career that lasted eighteen years in the NHL and four more in the World Hockey Association, we often played tennis together, and later golf. In fact, he was my doubles partner in the celebrity tennis events CBC used to air in the 1980s. The tournaments would include celebrities such as musicians Hagood Hardy and John Allan Cameron and filmmaker Norm Jewison, as well as hockey players including Frank, Eddie Shack, Ron Ellis, Vaclav Nedomansky and Henri Richard, among others. I actually won the tournament once, the last year it was contested.

What I learned about Frank as his tennis partner is that he never cared to take the lead. He was so laid-back and unaware of how phenomenally talented he was; he completely lacked a killer instinct. He'd have a chance to finish a guy off, but instead, he'd just hit the ball back to him. He seemed to enjoy the game and the play more than winning. Tennis is a thinking person's game; you need to hit every shot with a purpose. You have to be trying to kill with each shot. Not Frank, though. He'd just hit the ball — and beautifully. Still, I must say I thoroughly enjoyed having him as a partner.

After a brilliant junior hockey career with Toronto St. Michael's Majors, Frank skated directly into the NHL with the Maple Leafs. Although he joined the NHL the same year as Bobby Hull, the golden boy who had played junior in St. Catharines, it was Frank who made his mark first, scoring 20 goals and 36 points in 67 games to win the Calder Trophy as the league's top rookie.

Frank was consistent, if not spectacular, in his first three NHL seasons, but he took his game to a whole new level in his fourth year, when he finished third in league scoring with 48 goals and 84 points in 70 games. Frank was now officially a superstar.

With superstardom, though, comes pressure. And while Frank was a significant cog in a Leafs team that won three straight Stanley Cups beginning in 1961–62 and a fourth in 1966–67 — the last time Toronto won the Cup — he was not always a happy player. Frank told

me once he never felt like *the man* in Toronto. I don't even think
he realized he was a superstar. Toronto is the Mecca of the hockey
universe, and while other Maple Leafs have basked in the spotlight,
it seemed too much for Frank.

Not only that, but Leafs coach Punch Imlach made Frank his
personal whipping boy. Some star players can take being singled
out in front of their teammates, but Frank didn't have the appetite
for that. He would take it personally, and it made him withdraw
more and more into himself. Suddenly the game he loved to play,
and which he was so good at, became a living hell. I think Punch
wanted Frank to be a leader of the team, but that really wasn't his
nature.

Punch would deliberately mispronounce his name, calling him
Ma-hal-o-vich, and I think that drove Frank nuts. It was demeaning.
Frank Mahovlich was a dignified and proud man who could never do
enough to satisfy his coach. I think Frank would have been better off
without Punch as his coach, and that was proven when he moved on
to Detroit and Montreal.

If the Leafs didn't know what a great thing they had in The Big M,
others certainly did. The Chicago Black Hawks, for instance, offered
the Leafs $1 million for Mahovlich, a monstrous sum of money at the
time, but Toronto backed out of the deal. The Leafs did, however,
trade Mahovlich late in February 1968 as part of a blockbuster
deal that also sent Peter Stemkowski, Garry Unger and the playing
rights to Carl Brewer to the Detroit Red Wings for Norm Ullman, Paul
Henderson and Floyd Smith.

Frank told me he thought he'd be a Maple Leaf for life and was
absolutely shocked by the trade, but it turned out to be the best thing
for him, both personally and professionally. Toronto fans had taken
to booing the Big M, and he suffered. There was no pressure on him
playing in Detroit. Detroit offered him a fresh start, and it reunited
him with his brother, Peter. Skating on a line with Mr. Hockey,
Gordie Howe, and Alex Delvecchio, Frank soared to his greatest
heights as a player. During their first full season together as a unit,

Mahovlich, Howe and Delvecchio produced a whopping 264 points, and Frank scored a career-best 49 goals.

Even though the Red Wings had some of the greatest individuals who ever played in the NHL, they didn't come together as a very good team; during Frank's time in Detroit, they missed the playoffs in 1968 and '69. On January 13, 1971, Frank was on the move again, traded to the Montreal Canadiens for Guy Charron, Bill Collins and Mickey Redmond. Again, Frank found himself in a position where he could just go out and play and not worry about a leadership role. The Canadiens had leaders like Henri Richard and, in his final season, Jean Beliveau. It was with Montreal that Frank enjoyed two of his greatest triumphs, winning the Cup in 1970–71 and again in '72–73. Frank was a major contributor to both championship teams, scoring 14 goals and 27 points in 20 playoff games during the first Cup run and 9 goals and 23 points in 17 games during the second. I don't believe, having televised those series, that the Canadiens could have won without the Big M.

When Montreal beat out Boston in 1971, much of the credit went to the big, lanky rookie in the Habs' net, Ken Dryden. He played college hockey at Cornell and spent most of his first pro season with the American Hockey League's Nova Scotia Voyageurs before joining Montreal late in the regular season. Dryden played six games and instantly wrestled the number one goaltending job away from Rogie Vachon and Phil Myre. The big, bad Bruins, led by Bobby Orr and Phil Esposito, had easily finished first in the standings with a 57–14–7 record, 24 points ahead of Montreal, who posted a 42–23–13 mark. When they met in the first round of the playoffs, the Bruins — who had the league's top four scorers in Phil Esposito, Bobby Orr, Johnny Bucyk and Ken Hodge — were expected to roll over the Habs, but they were in for a surprise.

Dryden frustrated the Bruins at every turn. Naturally, because he seemed to have burst onto the scene from out of nowhere, Dryden was thrown into the spotlight by fans and media alike. For me, though, the series belonged to Mahovlich. Frank was playing what was arguably the best hockey of his life. Players who took part in that series will tell you it was the Big M, more than Dryden, who put the Habs over the top. To say merely that he was brilliant would be an understatement.

Some people mistook Frank's calm demeanour and smoothness on the ice for laziness. Was he trying as hard as he possibly could every game? Put it this way: opponents would often say, "Don't wake him up. Don't bother him" — he seemed to be a friendly giant until he got riled up, but once that happened, he could be quite ferocious. That didn't happen often enough. Many superbly talented athletes who make it look easy are often mistaken as indifferent. That was just as true of Frank.

I never cared what his critics said about him; to me, Frank Mahovlich was one of the most gifted skaters I ever saw. He was beautiful to watch, even in practice. If I had to pay money to watch two guys skate up and down the ice, it would be Frank and Bobby Hull. They made it look so easy.

Frank was a member of Team Canada in the Summit Series, but he wasn't really a big factor in the series. Remember, this was a very political time in our history, and to many, the Summit was much more than a hockey tournament; it was a clash of political lifestyles — capitalism versus communism. Frank was spooked by the Russians, particularly when the team travelled to Moscow for the final four games of the event. He swore the rooms were bugged, and it drove him to distraction. Turns out he was right: the rooms and the phones were discovered to have been bugged. I really felt during the games in Moscow that he wanted to go home, but he stayed.

When the WHA came into being, Frank took advantage of a golden opportunity to make some serious money. A number of stars, including Bobby Hull and Derek Sanderson, jumped to the rival league, only to eventually return to the NHL. For Frank, though, it marked the final chapter of his long career. He played two seasons with the Toronto Toros and two more after the team relocated to Birmingham.

It was obvious from the get-go that Frank didn't know much about his new league. I recall going out to dinner once with Frank and Dick Irvin, and he asked us, "Will I be going to California with this league? Who else is in the league? Does Chicago have a team?"

He didn't even know who the teams in the league were. Frank was funny that way.

Upon retirement, Frank was inducted into the Hockey Hall of Fame in 1981. He entered the world of politics in 1998 when he was appointed a senator by Prime Minister Jean Chrétien. I was very proud of my friend and happy for his wife, Marie.

I will always remember Frank as a great hockey player, but, without sounding too harsh, I don't think he ever reached his pinnacle. He never once scored fifty goals in a season, and I think he had the talent to score fifty many times over if he had really had more drive and desire. He is never mentioned when people talk about the top five players of all time, but in my heart I think that, had he played to his potential, he easily could have been one of the best, if not *the* best, ever. When I talk to the old players about guys they played with or against, only a few names bring that sparkle of appreciation in their eyes. And the Big M's is one of them.

As a friend who spent quite a bit of time with the Big M, I can tell you he was as sensitive, proud and intelligent an athlete as I have ever encountered. It just seems to me that hockey was not the singular most important thing in his life.

Fellow Hall of Famer Dick Duff once said of Frank, "It's not that he ever takes a night off; you just never knew when he was going to be really on."

Frank could do marvellous things on a hockey rink. It just didn't always seem to occur to him to do them.

Chapter 18

THE DYNASTY
GRETZKY, SATHER
AND THE OILERS

> "This kid is going to get killed in the NHL!" — *Hockey Night in Canada* analyst Howie Meeker, upon seeing Wayne Gretzky play his first NHL game

I'm like most of my fellow Canadians in that I have always had a great appreciation for Wayne Gretzky, both as a hockey player and as a person. I was also lucky enough to get to know Wayne and his family personally on a long-term basis.

Brian McFarlane was the first person to bring Gretzky to my attention. Brian had played an NHL old-timers' game in Hamilton in which Wayne played — and scored a goal — as a ten-year-old. He came back and said, "Ralph, you've got to see this ten-year-old kid named Wayne Gretzky. He's unbelievable! This kid is going to be a great player."

I was interested, but unimpressed, so we didn't do anything on him right away. But Brian kept pushing him as a story idea. When Wayne was twelve, playing with kids a few years older than him, Brian told me he had scored 378 goals for his local Brantford Nadrofsky Steelers. Imagine, nearly 400 goals in a season! Suddenly, everyone was talking about this little kid from Brantford with the white gloves who was scoring goals at a rate no one had in history — anywhere!

Finally — and I give Brian a lot of credit for it, because he was part of our creative team — we did a feature on Wayne for *Hockey Night in Canada*. Jack Dennett, who had been with *Hockey Night* since the 1930s, said, "Ralph, I can never remember the show doing a feature on the intermission on a twelve-year-old kid. Who is he?" To set things up, I had to call Wayne's dad, Walter Gretzky, and that marked the beginning of a relationship between him and me that has lasted over the years. Walter couldn't believe we were interested in doing a feature on his son, but in true Gretzky fashion he was more than co-operative. Walter and Wayne came to Toronto for a Maple Leafs game and we took a shot of them in the crowd.

When Wayne moved to Toronto as a fourteen-year-old to play with the Young Nats, I went to watch him. He was phenomenal — and he was playing against men five and six years older than himself. Like everybody else, I sat back and watched as the Gretzky legend grew. He went from being a superstar junior to a pro by the time he was seventeen. Of course, he turned pro with the World Hockey Association — and even though that league had lured Gordie Howe, Dave Keon and Bobby Hull to play in it, many of us still regarded it as a minor league.

When the Oilers joined the NHL in 1979, *Hockey Night in Canada* was scheduled to show their first home game on television. Wouldn't you know it, the opposition, the Detroit Red Wings, were fogged in and stuck in Vancouver and arrived forty-five minutes late. We had to fill all that time while we waited for them to show up. Once the game was finally underway, our analyst, Howie Meeker, after watching Gretzky skate his first few NHL shifts, piped up and said, "That kid is going to get killed in the NHL!" Howie's comments were a major story in the national press the following day.

At the same time that Gretzky was establishing himself as one of the greatest NHL players ever, I also had a friendship with Oilers coach and general manager Glen Sather that lasts to this day. In fact, I still regard Glen as one of my closest friends.

Looking back, it amazes me how our lives intertwined through the years ... the Gretzkys, Mellanbys and Sathers.

Early in Wayne's NHL career, I asked Glen if I could get Wayne to be a part of our "Pro Tips" feature with Meeker, but Glen said, "Would you please use Mark Messier instead?" Wayne got all the exposure, and he wanted Mark to get some attention, too. It went very well for us. Mark had such a great personality and attitude. And he was popular with the NHL All-Stars in the series, players like Larry Robinson and Mike Bossy.

In 1980, when the Islanders met Philadelphia in the Stanley Cup finals, I decided to bring my son, Scott, along for the series. It was a first. We had a bus travelling between the two cities, so he joined in on the fun. That year, I also flew Gretzky in to be a part of the telecasts. Wayne was quite a superstar by now and I thought he'd bring great attention to our game in Canada. To be honest, I also wanted to lend a little Canadiana to the series. During the game, Wayne sat with Scott and my wife, Janet. Afterwards, I asked Scott, who was thirteen at the time, "So, what did you think of Wayne Gretzky?"

Scott said, "I don't know ... I was too nervous to speak to him. He's a star!"

I could never have imagined at the time that, only a few short years later, Scott and Wayne would be facing each other in the Stanley Cup finals. The year after I retired from *Hockey Night in Canada*, 1986–87, was Scott's rookie year in the NHL. The Flyers met the Oilers in the Stanley Cup finals that spring, so I was obviously cheering for my son. Glen had won his Cups; now it was my son's turn. What a series it was — the Oilers taking it in seven games. The Flyers were a young, gritty team, but they wound up being no match for the Oilers dynasty.

At those finals, Walter would say, "Hey, Ralph, our kids are doing pretty good!" I thought to myself, "My kid is doing well — *yours* is phenomenal." What a regular, down-to-earth guy Walter was. And always happy ... always up. He had an innate sense of what the game is all about, and that's something I believe he passed on to Wayne.

I asked Walter once about the way Wayne could see the ice and anticipate the play, and Walter said, "I taught him." When Wayne was little, Walter said, he used to have a pointer, and when they watched games on television, he would tell Wayne to try to figure out where the puck was going to go — never mind watching where it was.

"I taught Wayne to always concentrate on what was going to happen next and to go to those areas," Walter said.

Before Game 7 of the finals, Scott and I had gone to lunch, and he told me he had a plan to clobber Wayne Gretzky.

"Dad, I'm going to tell you something — and don't tell Don Cherry or anybody," Scott said. "When Wayne comes in on my side, he always does a spin move, circling backwards. I've been watching tapes, and I'm going to knock him into the fourth row of seats."

"You know you'll have to fight Wayne's bodyguard, Marty McSorley, if you do that," I warned.

"I know, Dad," Scott said. "When Wayne starts to make his turn, I'm going to go towards the middle of the tight circle and I'm going to lay him out. This is Game 7. This is war!"

Late in the first period, sure enough, Wayne came down Scott's side and started his loop. Scott made his move … and missed Wayne by a mile! Not only that, but Wayne got a great scoring opportunity on the play. Philadelphia coach Mike Keenan sat Scott on the bench for most of the remainder of the game after that.

I recall sitting on the porch at Glen's house in Banff that summer. As usual, we were smoking our cigars. You'll never see Glen off the ice without a cigar in his mouth — even if he's only chewing on it.

Scott was with us, and he told Glen that story, then asked, "Mr. Sather, how could Wayne have known what I was going to do?"

Glen took a puff on his cigar and said, "Simple. Because he's Wayne Gretzky."

I also believe Walter instilled a lot of Wayne's creativity in him. They say you're born with that, but I'm not sure. I think Walter deserves a great deal of credit for teaching Wayne about the game, and I believe that Wayne listened carefully.

Everything Wayne became, I believe he owes to his parents. When a kid moves away to live — without his parents — in a strange city at the age of fourteen, he had better have received some good life lessons early to help him. Wayne once told me how tough it was to move away from home at such a young age. He's not an outgoing guy; he's pretty deep.

Even before the Oilers won their first Stanley Cup in 1984 (the first in a run of five championships in seven years), you could see how good they were going to be. They had youth and raw talent. And, of course, my pal Glen was the leader and a great coach. He knew how to treat the young players, and they respected him. A lot of the Oilers, including Wayne, would hang out in Banff, Alberta, in the summer. While I worked on the Winter Olympics in Calgary, I rented Glen Sather's coach house there. Glen, who is a great outdoorsman, tried to turn me into a "mountain man" ... without success. He took me cross-country skiing and taught me whitewater canoeing. He was a big kid in a lot of ways, and so was I. I loved our friendship and the wonderful times we spent on the golf course and tennis court.

Glen is one of the brightest, most inquisitive men I have ever been associated with. He is also one of the biggest practical jokers in history. Once, when we were whitewater canoeing down the Bow River from Banff to Canmore, he put me at the front of the canoe. By the end of the trip, I was so exhausted I could hardly stand up. That night, Glen and one of his buddies were laughing, and I asked, "What's so funny?"

Glen said, "The guy at the back just steers the canoe; the guy at the front does all the paddling."

That was typical of Glen's sense of humour. He's a trickster. Any trick he could play, he would play it.

Red Fisher, the great Montreal hockey writer, came to Glen's home in Banff, and he just loved the big painting of an Indian chief that Glen had hanging in his house. Red said he would love to have one like it, and Glen said, "I'll get you one, don't worry."

At the NHL draft one year, Glen decided to give Red his own

"Indian painting." At a cocktail party, with many friends on hand, he made his presentation, unveiling a framed photograph of NHL defenceman Jim Neilson, a Native Canadian, wearing a headdress, painting his home in Edmonton. Glen would always go that extra mile if it meant playing a practical joke on a friend.

The summer after the Oilers beat the Flyers in the '87 finals, I rented Glen's house in Banff. Well, I found Oilers Stanley Cup championship stickers everywhere I went in that house and beyond — even in my car. Glen had hidden them all over the place, knowing I'd find them.

Since we'd moved to Calgary and Banff, Scott got to know Glen like an uncle. The next thing I knew, in 1991, Scott was traded to the Oilers for Jari Kurri. I was thrilled — my son and a best pal in the same organization. Scott spent two years with the Oilers and played pretty well for Glen. After that, Scott was picked by Florida in the expansion draft, and Glen told me he was doing my son the best favour of his career by allowing him to go to a team where he would play more and be a leader. He knew the Oilers eventually would not be able to afford to keep Scott. Playing for Florida meant that Scott go to play in the finals a second time, in 1996, when the Panthers were swept by Colorado.

I was surprised that Edmonton didn't win more Cups. I thought that they could have won seven or eight, but Glen could foresee the way the money game was changing, and he knew he was not going to be able to keep all those young stars together. The Oilers simply could not afford to pay their players what they wanted, so they all had to be moved. It's really too bad. In my opinion, there will never again be dynasties in the NHL. It's too hard to keep a good team together, because of free agency and arbitration. Thanks, Gary Bettman!

The day Wayne was traded by Edmonton to Los Angeles, I was on the golf course with Alan Eagleson. It was a charity event Al ran each year. At the tenth hole, the media surrounded us, wondering about our opinion of the trade. I was shocked — I couldn't believe it. I would have bet 100,000 to 1 that Gretzky would play his entire career with the Oilers. Glen Sather had always told me that if he were ever forced to trade Wayne, they would have to trade him, too. But it was about big business, not loyalty. The Oilers were not going to be able to pay Wayne what he was worth, while the Kings could.

Wayne was the greatest offensive player ever, but he wasn't the total package the way Gordie Howe and Bobby Orr were. He was light and wiry, and he got away with a lot of stuff because he was protected. The only negative thing I ever heard about Wayne came from a lot of the refs, who said he used to complain and bark a lot about their calls. I hear the same thing about Sidney Crosby today. I guess their burning passion to win just gets the better of these players.

Near the end of his career, I bumped into Wayne after one of Scott's games, behind the arena in Florida where the team bus was parked. I said, "Wayne, the Rangers are struggling."

He said, "Mr. Mellanby, we are. Not only that — for me personally, every hit is starting to hurt."

Every player who ever told me something like that retired shortly afterwards. And Wayne was no exception. When you start bringing the pain from playing the game home with you, it's time to call it a career. There are more important things in life.

In later life, I was lucky enough to work with and get to know Wayne. My company did his Coca-Cola commercials, and Wayne told me that my television crew was the first to be allowed into his home. Later, we did a television pilot — *Wayne Gretzky and the Heroes of Hockey* — for a series that never happened, but not because of Wayne. He was wonderful and easy to direct. A similar series had come out, beating us to the punch.

Years ago, Glen invited me and some of my *HNiC* guys back to a bar in Edmonton owned by Mike Barnett. I liked Mike right away (and still do), never knowing he'd become Wayne's lifetime friend, agent and finally the general manager of the Phoenix Coyotes. It's a funny life.

That night, Mike — the restaurateur — said, "Ralph, someday I believe our friend Wayne will be more than just a player ... perhaps a coach or even an owner."

I said, "Mike, just be satisfied that he is one of the greatest players in NHL history. The other things will never happen."

Wrong again!

Let me tell you something about the Edmonton Oilers and their character guys. Once, I was speaking at a major management function, "The Business of Sport," and I looked down and there was defenceman Kevin Lowe.

"What are you doing here?" I asked. "You're a player."

Kevin replied, "Someday I want to be a GM; I'm here to learn."

Many players came to visit Banff in the summertime when I lived in Glen's coach house. One day, Glen introduced me to Craig MacTavish, formerly of the Boston Bruins. Because of his problems with alcohol and a jail sentence for vehicular homicide, Craig was *persona non grata* in the NHL. Harry Sinden and the Bruins had released him.

Later, as we smoked our cigars, Glen said, "Well, what do you think?"

I said, "Glen, that is a classy guy who made a mistake."

Sather signed MacTavish in February 1985, and the rest is history. MacTavish was a member of three of Edmonton's Cup-winning teams, and won another with the New York Rangers in 1994.

When the Oilers made the Stanley Cup finals in 2006, their general manager was Kevin Lowe, and the coach was Craig MacTavish. That ought to tell you, in a nutshell, how special those Oilers teams were, and it speaks volumes about the influence of Glen Sather and Wayne Gretzky, I'm sure.

Chapter 19

THE ENTERTAINER
BERNIE "BOOM BOOM" GEOFFRION

> "Boom Boom was the best singer who ever played for me — and he was also one hell of a good hockey player." — Toe Blake, Hall of Fame coach of the Montreal Canadiens

Bernie Geoffrion loved to be the life of the party.

That's one of the reasons why it stuck me as so sad that he passed away the very day before he was to be honoured by the Montreal Canadiens, who raised his Number 5 to the rafters at the Bell Centre. Bernie would have cherished the notion of standing before the Habs faithful and being acknowledged once and for all for his years of great service to the Montreal hockey scene.

Bernie told me that he never really felt his role as a member of the Canadiens team that won five Stanley Cups in a row, something no other organization has ever accomplished, was fully appreciated. Sure, the Canadiens had many great stars in that era — Rocket Richard, Jean Beliveau, Dickie Moore, Doug Harvey and Jacques Plante, to name a few — but Geoffrion was every bit as important to those championship teams as any of his teammates.

In fact, it could be argued that he was their best playoff performer. During the five-year Cup run, Geoffrion scored 29 goals and 68 points in 49 postseason games. In 1956–57, when Montreal won its second straight Cup, he led the team with 11 goals and 18 points in 10 games. If Geoffrion's name didn't carry the same cache as the Rocket's or Beliveau's, there was no denying his greatness. He was a First Team All-Star in 1961 and a Second Team All-Star in 1955 and 1960; he won the Hart Trophy as the NHL's most valuable player in 1961, led the NHL in scoring in 1955 and 1961 and was named the NHL's rookie of the year in 1952. He was inducted into the Hockey Hall of Fame in 1972.

Nobody loved the spotlight more than Boom Boom Geoffrion. Those who played with him in Montreal often said that if he got up in the middle of the night to get a drink, he'd do three encores when he opened the fridge door because the light came on. The man who has been credited with inventing the slapshot — hence the nickname "Boom Boom" — loved to entertain. He would belt out a tune at the drop of a hat and often kept his teammates in stitches with his comical routines. He loved to keep his teammates loose, be it in the dressing room, at the airport or in the lobby of their hotel on the road. The amazing thing is, he was just as entertaining as a player.

Bernie told me he used to work on his slapshot in practice. He discovered the shot by accident, and he loved it, but the legendary Canadiens coach Dick Irvin didn't care for it. Players mainly relied on the wrist shot back then.

"Dick Irvin used to tell me my slapshot wasn't accurate," Boom Boom told me.

"So why did you use it, then?" I inquired.

"It just came naturally to me. I could shoot the puck so hard. I have a wrist shot, too, you know. And a hell of a backhand shot, too. When I came up and played for Irvin, I just pretended I didn't understand English. He would tell me not to slap the puck and I would just look at him, pretending I didn't understand what he was saying to me. After a while, though, I won him over. Once the puck started going in the net, he told me he loved the slapshot. Then my English improved rapidly."

It's funny, but after Bernie and his family moved to Atlanta, in the deep south, everyone seemed to understand him — he spoke French-Canadian broken English with a southern accent!

I first got to know Boom Boom when he made his comeback with the New York Rangers in 1966. He had retired from the Canadiens a few years earlier, but he really missed the game. Knowing that he was going to play again, we at *Hockey Night in Canada* decided to put together an intermission segment about Boomer that would air between periods of his comeback game — scheduled, as luck would have it, against the Canadiens. Bernie was delighted at the notion of being before the cameras once again. You never had to ask him twice about having his life story told on television.

We filmed him at his home in Montreal and all over New York — even riding in a cab. It was a great piece. Of course, the night was made that much more special when, upon his return to the old Montreal Forum, he scored two goals and added an assist and was named the game's first star. It was a Hollywood ending for a player who was a consummate entertainer.

What was Geoffrion really like? I really got to know Bernie even better after the NHL expanded to Atlanta and the Flames named him their head coach. I was in Atlanta helping the team with their telecasts and had taken my wife, Janet, along for the trip. The Flames were slated to play the Washington Capitals at home and then again in Washington. I was also scheduled to go to Washington, so Cliff Fletcher asked Janet and me to join the team on their charter. Teams generally flew commercial back then; a chartered flight was the exception to the rule.

Janet, who was a small-town girl from Saskatchewan, had never been on a team flight before, and wouldn't it be just her luck that the Flames lost the first game of the back-to-back series with the Capitals? When we got on the plane, Bernie — as was his style — went out of his way to make Janet feel both welcome and comfortable.

"My dear Madame Mellanby, it is such a great pleasure to have you on our flight," he said in broken English. "We will sit up front in first class. I am just going to go to the back of the plane to tell the players not to bother us."

We were all alone when the flight took off. When Bernie rejoined us, he sat down and loudly announced, "I would like some champagne for Madame Mellanby." Then he turned to Janet and said, "Have you ever been to Washington? Wonderful place ... wonderful place."

They chatted ... Janet was quite charmed.

Bernie was in great form, especially after suffering such a tough defeat.

Then he turned to me with his game face on and said, "Did you see that goddamn game? Those fucking guys back there ... did you see that damned last goal? Did you see that shitty play?"

Janet was shocked! She said nothing, but gulped down the champagne.

That was Boom Boom Geoffrion. He had his lighter side, but he also had a burning desire to excel ... to be great. I know it crushed him inside that he never really had the impact as a coach that he desired. In 281 games behind the bench of the Flames, Canadiens and New York Rangers, Boomer had a 114–119–48 record. Truth be told, he never really had an overabundance of talent on the teams he coached; certainly not the talent he needed to win — and he wanted to win so badly. He would try to coax his players to be better. If he was coaching the expansion Flames in a game against Montreal, he would tell the players, "I've got to say, tonight we are playing the Canadiens, and I would not trade any one of you for any of their guys!"

Naturally, the players didn't buy it — the Canadiens had guys like Guy Lafleur, Larry Robinson and Serge Savard.

In practices, he would tell his Flames, "There are only three things you need to know about hockey: skate and check."

The guys would stand there waiting for him to name the third thing. It never came.

I came to love Bernie later in his life, after I moved to Atlanta. Although the Flames moved to Calgary in 1980, the NHL established another franchise in Atlanta in 1999, and my son, Scott, signed with the Thrashers in 2004 as a free agent. He was named the team's captain the following year.

People will tell you that the more Bernie likes you, the more he will make you the brunt of his wicked sense of humour. I know that only too well.

Once, Bernie came to a Thrashers practice to address the players — to give them a motivational speech. I happened to be at the rink that day, and when I spotted him, I said, "Bernie, do they let French-Canadians in here?"

Well, you should have heard him.

"This guy is the most overrated television producer in history," he bellowed through the rink. "He's in the Hockey Hall of Fame ... blah, blah, blah."

He really gave it to me — in front of my son and the team.

You should have seen Atlanta coach Bob Hartley howling with laughter. Boomer was one of his idols.

"They have his kid here and they make him captain. Let me tell you, it is because of the kid, not because of anything the old man ever did."

I was laughing so hard I had tears in my eyes.

That's Bernie. If he likes you, he really gives it to you. If he doesn't like you, he wouldn't give you the time of day.

Once, when a group of former Atlanta Flames players were getting together to have a surprise dinner for former broadcaster Jiggs McDonald, I got a call to join the party. My new wife, Gillian, didn't really want to attend with me, because she didn't know the guys, but I convinced her to come. She knew who Boom Boom Geoffrion was — hell, everybody knew who the Boomer was — and I was really excited for her to meet my old pal.

We walked into the restaurant and, wouldn't you know it, the first person we saw was Boom Boom.

"Bernie," I said, "I would like you to meet my wife, Gillian."

He took her hand, gently kissed it and said, "Madame, you have my condolences."

She couldn't get rid of him all night; he made her feel right at home.

I had gone through some boxes of memorabilia I had collected over the years and came upon a pair of gold cufflinks that had been given to me in 1968, the night the renovated Montreal Forum opened. They had the Canadiens' emblem on them. Once, while having lunch with my son, Scott, and Bernie, I took them out and said, "Bernie, I always wanted to give you these."

He said, "No, you can't, Ralph. I can't accept such a beautiful gift."

I said, "Take them. You earned them. All I did was TV."

I could tell by the look in his eyes he really treasured those cufflinks. In fact, I think he wore them in his casket.

I spoke with Bernie a few days before he died, and he told me, "Ralph, I will be there [for the sweater retirement ceremony]." Sadly, it wasn't to be. I'm glad, however, that in the years we both lived in Atlanta, we became close and shared time together.

Although Bernie never felt truly appreciated for his many accomplishments, I think he would have been deeply satisfied at the huge turnout at his funeral. Maybe the fans didn't hold him in high enough esteem, but those who played with and for him certainly did. It was a full house, including Jean Beliveau and many of his former players.

Boom Boom Geoffrion was one of a kind — a Hall of Fame player and a fantastic singer. He was a great personality, and a comedian to boot. He wasn't an easy guy to understand, but he was an easy guy to love. He epitomized fun — fun to play golf with, fun to talk with, fun to share life with.

I miss the Boomer.

OVERTIME
OFF-CAMERA

Chapter 20

THE LAST OF THE PIRATES HAROLD BALLARD

> "Mellanby, I lost your phone number … am I ever glad! Now I don't have to talk to you." — Harold Ballard, having a bit of fun, as usual, with Ralph Mellanby in the *Hockey Night in Canada* days

Just about everybody in the hockey world called him Pal Hal, but truth be told, I'm not sure Harold Ballard really had too many real pals, especially late in his life when he had grown into a crusty old curmudgeon. I will say, however, that I loved the old coot. I'm not suggesting he's the kind of guy I would have hung with, but I knew that, in my capacity as executive producer of *Hockey Night in Canada*, I needed my "Pal Hal" in my corner. He was both a powerful and an unusual force in the National Hockey League.

There are those who insist that, when he was the owner of the NHL's most valuable franchise, the Toronto Maple Leafs, he drove it into the ground. They insist he was a power-hungry, sadistic megalomaniac who was more interested in upsetting people — including those who faithfully paid to watch his team play — and keeping his name in the headlines than he was in building a winner.

The older Harold grew, the more irritable he got, particularly when it came to dealing with the media. He was the ultimate combination of stubborn, belligerent and unapproachable, but he still loved the spotlight. How ironic.

But I didn't see Ballard in quite the same light as most others did. The fact is, I treasured my relationship with Harold, who was both helpful to *Hockey Night in Canada* and a constant source of pure, unadulterated entertainment. I never saw Harold when he wasn't playing tricks on somebody. I swear he woke up every morning and said, "Whom can I have fun with today? Whom can I foul up today? Where's the action today?"

Born in 1903, the son of a wealthy manufacturer of ice skates, Harold said he was a champion speed skater, though I've found no record to support this claim. He wasn't particularly good at playing hockey, but he loved the sport and eventually managed the Maple Leafs' feeder teams. He joined the Leafs in 1957 to assist Stafford Smythe in running the organization, and then, in 1971, took over sole ownership of Maple Leafs Gardens Ltd. It is said that Ballard won a bitter battle for ownership of the team by sweet-talking a drunken Smythe into changing his will to leave the team to him. I don't believe this to be true. I do know — because I was present — that when Stafford lay in state, Harold tried unsuccessfully to pull him from the casket so they could have a final drink together.

In love with power, Ballard made sure everybody knew who was boss. When players became popular, he would chop them down at the knees. Hall of Famer Dave Keon, one of the greatest captains in Leafs history, has never forgiven the organization for the treatment he received from Ballard. Popular Leafs Darryl Sittler and Lanny McDonald were both traded away at the height of their careers.

Through it all, though, I felt a special bond with Ballard. And I'm certain that he, in his own weird way, liked me, too.

I remember one time when I was at the NHL's governors' meetings to make a brief presentation about rule changes, and Ballard was sitting at the end of the table. In the middle of my speech, he piped up and said, "Mellanby, is this going to take much longer? I have to go to lunch with a good-looking babe." He was putting you on all the time — giving you little shots. It was his nature.

Some people have this notion that he was nothing more than a silly old bugger who made mistakes — a lot of mistakes — but to me he was a fun guy to be around. He was "showbiz" and I was a showbiz guy. What I remember most about Ballard was that I could always depend on him to come through for me. In my business, finding somebody you could depend on was a rare feat.

* * *

You rarely saw Ballard when he wasn't with his best pal, King Clancy. They were like Frick and Frack. I remember having lunch with King one day when Harold dropped by our table. After a little banter, Harold walked away and King said, "You know, it's amazing, Ralph; that guy has been around hockey for fifty years and he hasn't learned a damned thing about the game."

Harold's big thing was giving everybody a nickname. Whenever he saw NHL president John Ziegler, he always called him "Shortypants." We'd be sitting together and he'd see Ziegler and cry out, "Hey, Shortypants, get over here!" I'm not sure many others had the nerve to speak to the president of the league in such a manner, but Ballard really didn't give a damn. He called my boss, Ted Hough, "Huff 'n' Puff." He was like a child in a lot of ways … like a big kid. Perhaps he never really did grow up.

He was perhaps the most unusual businessman I ever came across in my life. In any dealings I ever had with him, his fee was always $10,000. If we wanted to add another camera position, it was $10,000. If we wanted to park another truck outside Maple Leaf Gardens, it was $10,000. If somebody wanted to turn the lights on inside the Gardens, it was $10,000. If I wanted him to make an appearance for some reason, even for charity, it was that same $10,000. How can you run a ship like that? But that was Harold. He must have driven his business manager, Donald Crump, nuts. I once asked Mr. Ballard — that's the way I always addressed him, because my father taught me that you always addressed a president as Mister — "Why always ten grand? What's the rationale?"

He shot back, "Do you want the rationale to be twenty grand?"

I never asked about the fee again, and it always stayed at $10,000.

I knew how to deal with Harold. You meet with a lot of idiots and crazy people in television, so dealing with Ballard didn't bother me. I kind of liked that type of guy, and I truly loved Harold. I knew if I had problems, I could go to him. I wouldn't always win, but I'd get there.

If an owner — say, Ed Snider from Philadelphia, who remains a powerful man in the NHL — said we couldn't do something, Harold would jump right in and support me because he couldn't stand most of the other owners. Especially not Ed.

Although Ballard presented a gruff exterior, he was as sentimental as any other man. The day after his wife's funeral, he came to my private room inside the Gardens, closed the door and sat there and cried. I never forgot that moment.

"Ralph," he said, "I hope you never have to go through this."

Now, let's be honest: here was a guy who made some decisions when it came to his personal life that not everyone would agree with (he had a reputation as being something of a ladies' man), but he had a big heart. When his wife died, that famous gruff exterior melted away, even if only behind closed doors, and you could see and feel the pain he was going through. Not many people know that he went to her gravesite almost daily.

Harold frequently used to pop into my room in the Gardens — not during the game, not after, but before the game. My room was something of a sanctuary, but he was always welcome. I had also met the Leafs previous owner, Stafford Smythe, a few times, and I wasn't too impressed. I always thought Frank Orr put it best when he wrote, "Stafford always thought with his groin." The first question Stafford ever asked me was, "Hey, Mellanby, are you any good with the babes?" It's tough to be a pro when you're dealing with that.

* * *

I first met Harold in the early '60s, when I was still directing *Hockey Night in Canada*, and I knew little about him. I met him with Stafford Smythe and Ted Hough upstairs in Maple Leaf Gardens, and he really didn't say much. He didn't make much of an impression on me at all, other than that he seemed to be a big, lovable clown. Being the director of the show, I had no idea that one day I would have to do business with this future Hall of Fame owner. I do recall — and this never changed — that he was a weird dresser, and that first meeting was no exception. Today I would say that he was dressed by the tailor for Cirque du Soleil.

When I got the job as executive producer, I had to get to know the most powerful people in the NHL, and of course the primary ones were the owners of the Maple Leafs and the Montreal Canadiens. The Leafs were *the* franchise on *Hockey Night in Canada*, the cornerstone of the show and, even today, the biggest television ratings draw. Ballard had taken over the Gardens, and I knew that, to do my job to the best of my ability, I needed him to play ball with me. I found out that he would go downstairs to the players' room, where the guys were treated for injuries, and take a daily sauna. He loved saunas. That was his method of keeping in shape — sweat it out.

Harold would always go downstairs for a sauna on Wednesdays and Saturdays (the days when the Leafs played home games) at 5 p.m., so I would go down and join him. I think after a while he kind of looked forward to my visits. That was when he would open up and tell me stories. He was a great storyteller and he shared a lot of inside stuff with me. He told me that the first day after he and Stafford bought the Gardens, they had Conn Smythe's private entrance bricked up. Smythe kept his office inside the Gardens, but Ballard had the private entrance covered. According to Harold, Smythe went nuts.

"I let that son of a bitch know where he stood," Ballard laughed.

On another occasion, he told me about the time he got into it with Jim Norris, the legendary owner of the Chicago Blackhawks. His father was James Norris Sr., owner of the Detroit Red Wings from 1932 to 1952 and the man after whom the Norris Trophy, awarded annually to the top defenceman in the NHL, is named.

It was James D. Norris, the son, whom Harold had dealings with. He once told me, "Ralph, I've got a story about Norris that the press doesn't know."

Of course I was intrigued, and Harold trusted that I wouldn't put it on television, so he told it.

There was an NHL governors' meeting in New York, and he and Stafford went up to Norris's apartment at the Waldorf Towers for a few nightcaps. Norris dismissed his bodyguard. The same trio had sent shock waves through the hockey world in October 1962, when Norris offered the Leafs $1 million for Frank Mahovlich's contract. Harold and Stafford accepted, but the deal fell apart the next morning when Conn Smythe told Tommy Ivan, who was set to deliver the cheque, the deal was off. On this occasion in New York, Norris and Stafford were both a little drunk, and they got into a fist fight. Harold told me he was pretty sober, so he went over to try to break things up.

"I pushed Big Jim into the fireplace," he said.

Well, Norris was so plastered that he fell down and hit his head on the fire grate and lay there motionless. There was blood all over the place, and Harold reached down to feel his pulse.

"There was no pulse," Harold recalled. You could tell, as Harold retold the story, that he was deeply concerned about what had happened.

"Stafford, what should I do?" he cried.

"Get his wallet!" Smythe said.

Thank God Big Jim then awakened. After he got cleaned up, they shared a few more drinks and laughs.

Once, Harold was seeking an extra million dollars in rights fees from *Hockey Night in Canada*. After much discussion, and no million, he brought my boss, Ted Hough, into his sauna and barred the door with a hockey stick so that Ted couldn't get out. Ted hated heat, but Harold was strong and could stay in the sauna for hours.

"I don't care if you stay in here until you turn into a prune," Ballard bellowed. "You're not getting out of here until I get my $1 million."

Ted had to give in or he would have died!

How I hated it when Harold built his own sauna upstairs in his apartment in the Gardens.

When he was cutting a local television deal with CHCH in Hamilton in 1977, Harold and the two owners of the television station were sitting in a restaurant across from the Gardens waiting for Ted. CHCH had already made the deal, buying the Leafs' local television rights away from CFTO in Toronto, without Ted being there.

When my boss arrived, Harold said, "Sit down and have something to eat."

"I don't want anything to eat," said Mr. Hough.

"You've got to have something to eat."

"Why?"

"You'll need something in your stomach to throw up when I tell you about the deal I just made, and how much it'll cost you!"

I don't see any characters in the game today who are bigger than, or as interesting as, Harold was. Whether he was right or wrong, he was fun. He was the last pirate.

* * *

Today, some members of the press say Harold was a terrible owner for the Leafs, but he was a good owner for me because I cared only about television. It didn't make a difference in the world to me whether or not his team enjoyed success. Win or lose, the Leafs were the NHL's biggest cash cow. It has been said the Leafs could hold their games at 3 a.m. in the middle of a blinding snowstorm and every seat would be sold and filled.

I thought the mistakes he made with the team were horrendous, and his business fee always being $10,000 was a joke. But none of that mattered to me. I cared only about my show and my people.

Harold always helped me by allowing me to do end runs around the league's powers that be. He was the king and he loved games — anything outside the accepted boundaries. He was the powerhouse, even when the Leafs were lousy. But if I told Mr. Ballard I had a problem, he was there for me, especially if he felt it disadvantaged the other NHL clubs.

Harold would never flat-out refuse me anything, but there were times when he would say, "If I do this for you, what are you going to do for me?" I knew what was coming: more charity requests. For instance, there might be the children's relief fund coming up, or a drive to raise money for cancer. I was always happy to help his causes, and there were many.

One of the most memorable chapters in the Harold Ballard saga transpired in March 1979, when he fired coach Roger Neilson, only to rehire him a day later. Neilson was wildly popular in Toronto, but the team was not doing well, so Ballard, who was impatient, canned him.

We planned a real show-business opening to our broadcast that night — Dave Hodge, our host, was going to stand outside the Leafs' dressing room to see who came out as the team's new coach. It was a question all of Canada was asking, and we would be the ones to answer it on national television.

I went downstairs for a sauna around four o'clock in the afternoon, and there was Roger. At that point, nobody knew where he was — he hadn't been at the team's morning skate — but there he was, hiding out in the sauna room.

Roger was his typical self: calm, cool and relaxed. I told him about our plans for the opening and the unveiling of his replacement as coach. Neilson answered, "It's me. I'm coaching tonight, but I've been sworn to secrecy."

I asked if there was some big ceremony planned or anything to mark his return to the team, and he said there was not.

"I won't be on the bench for the warm-up," Neilson said. "I'll just show up to start the game."

Harold wanted Neilson to arrive behind the bench wearing a brown paper bag over his head — like the Unknown Comic, a recurring guest on television's *The Gong Show* — and then take it off to surprise the crowd. Neilson, who loved a good laugh, almost took the bait, but after speaking with friends he decided that to do so would hurt his credibility. So there was no paper bag, but a surprise entrance was on the agenda.

I thanked Roger for telling me that, because it saved me and the rest of the crew at *Hockey Night in Canada* a lot of work, and gave him my word that I wouldn't let the cat out of the bag.

But I still had a television show to produce. And now that I had this valuable information, I had to act on it. I called the three guys I trusted most — director Ron Harrison, producer Bob Gordon and host Dave Hodge — out of their production meeting and into my room. I told them I knew that Neilson was coaching that night, so we shouldn't bother going to a lot of trouble with pre-production speculation. They didn't believe me. It's probably the only time they didn't believe me on anything, and I think it was because they were so pumped up at the prospect of having a spectacular opening to the show; if what I was telling them was true, it meant the broadcast was going to be anticlimactic.

The verdict: "On with the preplanned opening."

That night, out came Roger and up went the ratings — to record levels, thanks to Mr. Ballard.

Then there was the classic Christmas show.

I had promised Harold one year that he could be on the post-game segment at Christmastime. Harold had never been on the Christmas Eve broadcast before, but he wanted to make a pitch for his annual Christmas for Kids Foundation.

Hodge, who was hosting, asked Harold the very first question: "What are you going to give your coach for Christmas?"

"I'm going to give him a case of venereal disease," Harold said.

I couldn't believe it! I turned to Red Storey, who was playing Santa Claus, and said, "You've got to get in there and save us."

As Red made his way into the studio, dressed as Santa, Harold looked up and said, "What are *you* doing here, you old fart?" It went downhill from there. Thank heaven it was 10:30 p.m. and many of the kids were already in bed.

You talk about getting ratings! The Leafs were so lousy in those days that you needed *something* to sell the broadcast. And Harold was that something for us, even if he walked a dangerous line sometimes.

The next day, our phones were swamped with calls from angry viewers, and we received thousands of letters of complaint.

* * *

When I was having differences about the show at the executive level with my boss, Ted Hough, I would go see Harold. Most will remember that Harold had a special box at the north end of Maple Leaf Gardens, just behind the goal, where he sat during games. I would go and see him and make sure that the cameramen got a shot of the two of us sitting together. It would drive Ted nuts, and Harold knew it. What the hell I was doing with Harold and what were we discussing? I would do it only occasionally — but it would always work in my favour.

The thing that I admired about Harold was that he was the only owner in the NHL who attended every league function. He was at every Stanley Cup final and every All-Star Game, and he'd call me to make sure I knew where he was going to be sitting in the crowd.

"Make sure you get a shot of King and I," he would say. "These are our seat numbers."

Strange, he would never sit in a private box — always in among the fans.

He felt that every owner should attend the Stanley Cup finals and the All-Star Game. He felt it was important to do that. He had a real loyalty to the game and to the NHL.

He even went to Russia during the 1972 Summit Series — and that was the year he was going to prison for embezzling money from Maple Leaf Gardens Ltd. He was found guilty on forty-eight of fifty charges and sentenced to serve three concurrent three-year terms. He wound up spending one year in a minimum-security prison that he jokingly referred to as a "country club." I never figured out how he got out of Canada, but there he was in Moscow.

The other thing I admired about him was his charity work. Even if you didn't like him, or he drove you nuts, there was no denying he looked out for the little guy.

Harold said he looked at me as a nice guy, and knew that if he did a favor for me, it would be repaid.

The only time I ever said no to Harold was when we taped the popular intermission segment called "Showdown in the NHL" at the Markham Arena. It was basically a penalty-shot contest featuring some of the NHL's best snipers, and it was to run during intermissions on *HNiC* over the 1979–80 season. Alan Eagleson, executive director of the NHL Players' Association, told the players they could participate. And we had arranged with the league for the players to appear in their team uniforms.

I was producing the thing, and I'd lined up stars from all the other NHL teams. From Toronto, I wanted Darryl Sittler, Lanny McDonald, Ian Turnbull and goalie Mike Palmateer. But Punch Imlach, who had just returned to the Leafs, didn't want any of his players involved. He wanted to show Darryl Sittler and Lanny McDonald that he — and not the NHLPA — was the boss.

I asked Eagleson, "What's this about the Leafs not participating? They play in our biggest market."

"The Leafs will be there," Al insisted.

The phone rang in the television mobile unit; it was Ballard, and I'm certain that Punch was with him.

"I am ordering you to walk away and not produce the show!" he said.

Now, this was a multi-million-dollar feature, with the endorsement of our sponsors, which was to run as part of *Hockey Night in Canada* — *my* show.

"Mr. Ballard," I said, "I can't do that. I have to do my job."

"If you go through with this, you'll never walk into the Gardens again."

"I'm sorry," I said. "Talk to Mr. Hough."

He hung up.

Of course, he never followed through with that threat. In the end, the Leaf players were allowed to participate, but whenever a segment featuring a Leaf was to run, it wasn't shown in Ontario. We capitulated on this point, probably because we had no choice, but it really hurt the show.

I have always said that the "Showdown in the NHL" fiasco led to the demise of the Maple Leafs. They had a good team, but Imlach messed things up. He had recently returned to the Leafs after running the Buffalo Sabres, and while I can't speak for Punch, I think his attitude was "I'm going to show these bastards who is boss." He traded McDonald, and Sittler wasn't allowed to appear on *Hockey Night in Canada*. Ultimately, Sittler was traded, too.

Despite our ups and downs, for the most part Harold and I liked one another. I was with him when he laid his pal King Clancy to rest. Just before they closed the casket, Harold put a *Racing Form* inside King's jacket. Their other close friend, sportswriter Dick Beddoes, who was a bit of a cheapskate, tucked five dollars into King's pocket.

"You never know," Beddoes said. "They might have racing up there."

We all shared a laugh.

Our good relationship helped the show. Harold was constantly trying to fire Dave Hodge, trying to oust Brian McFarlane, trying to influence and control *Hockey Night in Canada*, but because of our relationship, we always seemed to solve the problems — or at least skirt them.

He was a great defender of Don Cherry, and he saved Don's broadcasting career.

At one time, Peter Maher (who is short) and Bob Cole (also small in stature) were doing play-by-play for the Leafs, on radio and television respectively. As a joke, Mr. Ballard asked me, "Why do you always hire these midgets from the East Coast?"

Since both Peter (who went on to do play-by-play for the Calgary Flames) and Bob are in the broadcast section of the Hockey Hall of

Fame, they are no midgets, and neither was Harold Edwin Ballard.

Late in his life, particularly after he bought the Canadian Football League's Hamilton Tiger-Cats, Harold changed dramatically. He became forgetful and more distant. In fact, when I went to work as head of the Canadian Football Network, I was at a meeting of the CFL's board of governors, and I don't think Harold even recognized me. I felt really bad for him. He was a sick man by this time.

When Harold died, he lay in state at Maple Leaf Gardens, and I stood in the long lineup to pay my respects. Harold's son, Bill Ballard, pulled me out of the line and brought me to the front. There were probably a thousand people ahead of me who were mad about this, but I followed him nonetheless.

I turned to Bill and said, "You know, I owe a lot to your dad. He did a lot for me."

"You know what, Ralph?" he replied. "You did a lot for him, too."

Chapter 21

TWO PRESIDENTS AND A COMMISSIONER

Throughout my career, dealing with the people who control hockey's fate has come with the territory. Sometimes these encounters have been pleasant, sometimes intimidating, sometimes infuriating (and in the case of Harold Ballard, a little of each!). This chapter will take a look at three of the men who have headed up the NHL since I started at *Hockey Night in Canada.*

CLARENCE CAMPBELL ALWAYS FOLLOW YOUR VISION AND RESPECT THE RULES

Clarence Campbell — or Mr. Campbell, as everyone called him — was the very model of a league president. In fact, I think that there were days when he thought he was the president of the United States! He commanded respect, and he received it. He also knew whom he worked for — the owners — and never went against them. Never.

I had a great run with Campbell and really enjoyed my time with him. We worked well together because I think he really understood what I was trying to do to bring a more journalistic slant, as well as a focus on entertainment, to *Hockey Night.* That isn't to say there weren't many bumps along the way, but for the most part I felt as though he had an appreciation of my work and my vision and how it could help the NHL.

I used to socialize with Campbell, too, and we even played a little golf together. Golfing with Clarence Campbell was an experience. I love the sport, but I'm also one of those golfers who, if my ball lands in a divot or I have a bad lie, will give it a little kick so I have a better shot. In other words, I play by winter rules all year round. But not when I golfed with Clarence. I tried it once and he gave me hell!

"Mr. Mellanby," he said, "that is not within the rules of golf. Don't ever do that when playing with me on my course."

He was dead serious. It was as if I were on trial for gambling or something.

Whenever we golfed and had others in our group, I would always warn them not to screw around, because Clarence would be watching them like a hawk and he'd call them on anything. I never invited my pal Ken McKenzie (the founder of *The Hockey News*) to join our foursome, because he was another fun-loving guy who was notorious for his indiscretions on the course.

Clarence was president of the Beaconsfield Golf Club in Montreal. He had a lake built right by the eighteenth hole because he felt the course needed a water hazard. I took former NHLer Ralph Backstrom and Dick Irvin there once, and after a few "pops" — and after it got dark — Ralph tossed his clubs right into Clarence Lake. He came back, had a few more pops and then went back to try to get them out — wading in successfully, while Dick and I killed ourselves laughing. Years later, after Campbell had passed away, I went back to televise an LPGA event, and Clarence Lake was still there.

Born in Fleming, Saskatchewan, in 1905, Campbell graduated from the University of Alberta with a bachelor's degree in 1924 and a law degree two years later. He won a Rhodes Scholarship to attend Oxford University in England, and while there he played for the famed Oxford Blues hockey team. Upon returning to Canada, he was called to the bar in Alberta — and hired as an NHL referee. He also officiated at Allan Cup games and in the American Hockey League.

In 1940, Campbell enlisted in the militia and received a commission in the Canadian Army shortly thereafter, rising through the ranks to become a lieutenant-colonel. While in Europe, he was appointed to the Canadian War Crimes Investigation Unit and was one of the lawyers assigned to the trial of Nazi general Kurt Meyer. For his efforts, he was awarded an MBE (Member of the Order of the British Empire) and made King's Counsel.

Before the death of the NHL's first president, Frank Calder, there had been rumours that Campbell was in the running to succeed him. Campbell rejoined the league in 1946 as assistant to president Mervyn "Red" Dutton. A few months later, Dutton resigned and Campbell took over as president, a post he remained in for the next thirty-one years.

Although he consistently sided with the owners, he was no pushover. This was never better illustrated than in March of 1955, when Montreal Canadiens superstar Maurice "Rocket" Richard lost his temper during a March 13 game, high-sticking Boston's Hal Laycoe in the face, causing a five-stitch cut, and then getting into a tussle, ultimately punching linesman Cliff Thompson. Campbell suspended Richard — who was leading the league in scoring — for the rest of the season, including the playoffs, costing Richard the Art Ross Trophy and, in all likelihood, costing his team the Stanley Cup.

Courageously, Campbell attended the next game at the Montreal Forum, on the 17th, and took his usual seat. That night, fans rioted, starting first in the arena and then flowing out into the streets of Westmount. Campbell, to his credit, did what he thought was right. He faced the tumult and the fury.

When Campbell first took control of the NHL, he moved quickly to raise the league's profile, extending the regular season from fifty games a year to sixty, then to seventy, introducing an annual all-star game and initiating the NHL pension fund with contributions from the players and owners. He was so proud of "his" pension fund that he ended every NHL function with a pension report — what a bore!

He was already a legend by time I met him. Over the years, I knew how our conversations would go by the way he addressed me on the phone. If he said, "Ralph…," I knew he wanted a favour from me. But when he said, "Mr. Mellanby…," I knew I was in trouble — and he could be quite an intimidating man. But fair — always fair.

The first time he ever referred to me as "Mr. Mellanby" was after Brian McFarlane commented during a broadcast that Forbes Kennedy, who hit a linesman, would be suspended. It turned out Brian was right, but Campbell didn't like a television announcer speculating on whether or not the league would punish a player.

I had to go to Campbell's office with tapes of the broadcast, and thank heavens my boss, Ted Hough, backed me — I really appreciated that. It was the first time I really needed his support, and I got it. Hough told Campbell, "I think you should be congratulating this young man for what he has done for the NHL and television and not bringing him in here to be criticized." Clarence respected Ted and backed off — but with a warning to McFarlane, which I did not deliver.

I really liked Mr. Campbell and felt I could read him pretty well. He was from the old school. He may not have liked all the things I was doing and trying to accomplish, but he always told me the same thing: "If it's good for hockey and it's good for the NHL, I'll back you." He was also a good friend of my uncle, Henry Mellanby, who was president of the Hudson's Bay Company, so there was some background there.

You have to remember that the NHL was a pretty small operation in Campbell's day. It's not like today, when the league has hundreds of employees working out of various locales. He ran the league out of an office in Montreal, with just a handful of additional staff in New York. I think that Campbell saw that the game had to grow, which led to the expansion that began in 1967, but there was never any mistaking who was in charge. In time, Campbell also moved to expand the league's administrative and — especially — marketing departments.

One of the things that always made me laugh was the fact that he insisted on running all the league meetings by himself, rather than delegating responsibilities. He was brilliant, but sometimes he'd mess up. During the first expansion draft, for instance, he got several of the new teams' nicknames wrong. He'd step up to the microphone and say, "The first choice goes to the Los Angeles Blades," instead of the

Los Angeles *Kings*. It was hilarious.

I used to ask his assistant, Brian O'Neill, who was a good orator, why he didn't run the meetings, and he'd say, "Oh, no — that's Mr. Campbell's territory."

Later, Brian did take over these functions and he did a great job — no more laughs. I was, and still am, a great admirer of Brian O'Neill, who complemented Clarence in a great many endeavours.

What was President Campbell like? Well, Frank Selke and I were in Boston on one occasion, and as we walked down the hallway of our hotel, we noticed that the door to Campbell's suite was open. He invited us in for a drink and we spent about two and a half hours with him. That's when he told me the story about suspending three players for gambling in 1946: Billy Taylor, Don Gallinger and Babe Pratt. He banned Taylor and Gallinger for life, but only gave Pratt a seventeen-day suspension (effectively sidelining him for nine games).

"The other two gentlemen lied to me," he explained. "We had the evidence, but I gave them the chance to tell the truth, and they said they didn't gamble. Babe Pratt came in, and when I asked him if he had been gambling, he said, 'I sure have, Mr. Campbell, and I'm making a piss-pot full of money.'"

Campbell told him that was not allowed, to which Pratt responded, "I don't gamble on *my* games; I gamble on other team's games and other sports."

Pratt pointed out that many of the team owners were connected with gamblers, especially through horse racing and boxing, but Campbell said, "None of that — nine games."

Babe told me he really didn't see anything wrong with betting on games he wasn't involved in, but he accepted his suspension and got on with his career. I think that if Taylor and Gallinger had admitted to gambling, they would have gotten off with a much more lenient punishment. From that point on, neither one of those guys liked Pratt because he got off easy. They never forgot, and they never forgave Campbell.

Clarence was a straight shooter, and his dealings with me were never anything but fair. Television was not his bailiwick, and I rarely put him on the air because he didn't come across well. He was too droll — not charismatic in any way, shape or form. I often asked O'Neill to speak about league matters, and by contrast, he was great on television.

I once asked Campbell, "I know you like what we're doing, but how do you like the French show?"

He said, "I don't watch the French show."

He didn't speak French, or at least didn't understand it well.

Bill Mazur hosted the games broadcast on CBS, and Campbell didn't care for his presentation. Mazur, who is still a star on radio in New York, had the idea that he was going to reinvent the wheel when it came to reporting hockey on television.

I told Bill, "Some of your ideas may go over in New York, but I don't think the NHL will like them. And I don't think you'll last too long in this league."

He said the games needed more pizzazz, and to some degree, he was right. He'd show the standings on television, but he'd say things like, "Let's take a look at the money board." When he put up a graphic showing the scoring race, he'd call it something like "the guys-who-don't-check race." Stuff like this made Campbell furious.

Mazur had asked me if his wife could come into my television room at the Montreal Forum to watch him work, and I said it was fine with me. Then Campbell came into the room, and I could tell he'd had a drink or two. When Mazur said, "Let's take a look at the money board," Campbell shook his head and said, "This man is a disgrace. Why do they have him on? He's terrible."

Then he turned and walked out of the room.

Well, Mrs. Mazur, who was a lovely lady, turned to me and asked, "Who is that terrible man?"

"He's just some guy who works at the Forum," I lied. I didn't want to tell her that the president of the National Hockey League had just taken a run at her husband. Nor did I want her to be in a position to tell her husband that the president of the league thought he was a disgrace — although, knowing Bill, he would have just eaten it up.

For my own part, I knew what I could do and what I couldn't do during Campbell's reign. I also knew how highly he thought of me, which was flattering. And, as I gained experience and power, I think he finally gave up on calling me and complaining about the show. McFarlane would say his piece and Dave Hodge would do his thing, and Mr. Campbell would just let me run the show. And when anybody complained to him about *Hockey Night in Canada*, he would simply say, "Mr. Mellanby is doing a good job. Leave him alone; leave him to me."

Clarence Campbell taught me a lot, not the least of which was what to expect from a president.

JOHN ZIEGLER THE VISIONARY

I knew John Ziegler very well before he took over as president of the NHL in 1977, having golfed with him at the annual NHL golf tournament in Vermont when he was a lawyer working for the Detroit Red Wings. Once, I nearly conked him on the head with a ball at the tournament — what better way to get acquainted? We remain friends to this day. I like to think we helped one another, and also helped the game.

In my opinion, Ziegler was generally underestimated; he never really received his just due. Not that I couldn't have continued working with Campbell and his people, but I saw Ziegler as a breath of fresh air who brought in a lot of new ideas and built up the New York office. He had a flair for promotion and marketing, and his first moves were in that direction. He supported Brian O'Neill — appreciated him and, surprisingly, kept him on as his assistant. He made O'Neill the NHL's operations man. Ziegler also aided Don Ruck by supporting much larger marketing, television and merchandising budgets. Later, he added Steve Ryan, a marketing whiz, and I loved creating and working with Steve on new ideas.

John and I were roughly the same age, and both educated in Michigan — I had graduated from Wayne State in Detroit and he was an alumnus of the University of Michigan. We both grew up not far from Detroit — he was from Grosse Pointe and I was from Essex, the village across the river.

Ziegler was a person who would listen, which I really appreciated. I was asked to attend the first meeting regarding the NHL Network, which was being formed at the time in the United States. I remember him talking to the crew at a dinner, saying, "I don't want anything disparaging said about the NHL on TV. This is a promotional tool for us." It was all stuff I didn't believe in. I believe in reporting, honesty and innovation. I had been fighting for the previous ten years to move forward. Ziegler was new, and he was wrong.

So I stood up and said, "Mr. Ziegler, these are television people and we're not going to do what you just said. We are going to report accurately and criticize when we have to. Television is not an NHL house organ."

Ziegler didn't say a word. Now, if that had been Gary Bettman, the NHL's current commissioner, he would have had my job. He would have said, "Get that guy out of here."

John was new, and he took the criticism with dignity, even though he didn't like it. That convinced me that he was a real man.

When I had new ideas, I could go right to John. I don't know if you could do that in today's league. I'd say, "What do you think about putting the draft on *Hockey Night* — and we'll get the sponsors for it?" He said, "Go for it." We had a really good, solid relationship. He would say, "Give it to Steve Ryan; we'll make it work."

Ziegler was a true sportsman. He played softball with us and he'd play hockey with the Hockey Knights. He was a hell of an athlete. That was one big difference between Ziegler and Campbell and Bettman: he could play. He had been a hockey player in college, and was a great tennis player and a good golfer, too. I know, because I played all those sports with him. I loved John because he was a real jock. He also loved and respected the NHL players, and I know they liked him.

Once, at the Bob Cole Tournament in Newfoundland, John spotted my boy, Scott, and me. The two of them started commiserating in a corner of Cole's house. I asked Scott, who had never spent time with John before, and who was also the player rep for the Philadelphia Flyers, "What did he tell you?"

"He sure asked a lot of questions," Scott said. "I was impressed."

I don't think people remember that he was the one who made the deal bringing the World Hockey Association teams into the NHL, which put more teams in Canada. Instead of fighting with Alan Eagleson, head of the NHL Players' Association, he collaborated with him for the good of the game. I'm not sure they always collaborated in the right way, but I still felt it was right to start working *with* the Players' Association rather than always fighting with them, the way Campbell did. That led to labour peace and league stability.

Everything Ziegler did, I happened to like. In fact, he asked me in the late '70s to put a group together to talk about the rules of the game as they applied to television. I brought in people who weren't tied to a team or the league, and we came up with a set of proposed rules. It is amazing that most of the rules we suggested are the same as or similar to those Brendan Shanahan and his group, the NHL's competition committee, came up with following the lockout in 2004–05.

I presented our rules proposal to Ziegler before he presented it to the NHL Board of Governors, and I told him there wasn't a single rule in the package that didn't already exist in the league's rule book. We wanted the league to implement the shootout to end tie games, but when you think about it, the penalty shot rule was already in effect. We also wanted no-touch icing, which is used in international and junior hockey.

The biggest change we wanted was for teams to be allowed to change lines only on the fly, but that one got killed by some of the not-too-bright coaches around the league. It got a trial in pre-season play, and the good coaches — guys like Scotty Bowman and Don Cherry — loved it, because they saw the advantage of being required to out-think their opponents. Cherry told me that in an exhibition game where the league tried the "change on the fly" rule, his players were sweating and really on their toes. Don liked that. Looking back, I think it would have created more scoring, because it's a lot harder to play defence than it is to play offence. It would also have sped up the game for television. Roone Arledge, the president of ABC Sports, Scotty Connal from NBC and the legendary Bill McPhail, then of CBS and later of CNN, all agreed that we needed a two-hour show in the United States. John asked me how we would get the commercials into the broadcast, and I told him that we'd have them after stoppages in play, and at scheduled intervals, which is how they do it now, thirty years later. I had all the network television guys on my side, but none of it came to fruition.

I was shocked. Not one of our rules was adopted. I know Ziegler was disappointed when the GMs and governors turned them all down. I guess the one thing that disappointed me was that Ziegler didn't have the power to sway the governors — he answered to them, just as Mr. Campbell had done.

The NHL wonders why it is having trouble getting the game to succeed on U.S. network television. But the problem is ongoing: the league asks television people for advice, then the owners don't listen.

Ziegler used his experience in business and as a lawyer to help solve a players' strike in 1992, but the owners weren't happy with the deal he cut and forced him to step down after the playoffs. It was a mistake to let Ziegler go — and then they compounded matters by replacing him with Gil Stein. Gimme a break! I thought Stein was a good man, just not a president. Stein will be remembered for trying — and failing — to get himself inducted immediately into the Hockey Hall of Fame; he didn't last the year and was replaced by Gary Bettman.

To me, Ziegler was a class act. In his final year, *Sports Illustrated* ran a cover story calling hockey the "sport of the future." Ziegler had the game positioned pretty well. He was a big believer in the international game and I think that, had he stayed, we would have NHL teams in a European division today. Think of the television revenue *that* would have brought to the league! To this day, John will never criticize the league, its teams or his successor. But, confidentially, I hope someday to have a golf game or tennis match with him, share a couple of beers and dream about what might have been.

GARY BETTMAN THE REIGN OF ERROR

In my opinion, if hockey was the sport of the future under Ziegler, it is close to being the sport of the past under Gary Bettman. I call his time as commissioner of the NHL (the league changed the job title when he took office on February 1, 1993) a litany of mistakes.

Bettman and I have not gotten together many times over the years, but every time we are in each other's company we have an argument. It started when I worked as a consultant with the Atlanta Thrashers when they entered the league in 1999. I don't know how he would have reacted had I become president and governor of the New York Rangers, which I very nearly did. But that's another story.

The first events I attended representing the Thrashers were television meetings in Nashville. Bettman gave a state-of-the-union address to all the television people and everybody applauded, though I thought that what he said about the game being in terrific shape was a bunch of baloney. He asked if anyone had anything to say, so I stood up and said, "I don't think the game is in as great a shape as you think it's in."

I talked about the hooking and holding and all the fighting. Bettman was livid. He does not like to be taken to task. Quite a contrast from John Ziegler!

I really don't speak with Bettman anymore, and I am certain he doesn't miss our conversations.

Gary Bettman's record as NHL commissioner is spotty at best. He got the league into more American markets, but most of those markets have not embraced the game, and as far as television is concerned, hockey is on weaker footing than ever before. I think the league's

American expansion under Bettman has been at the expense of Canadian markets. When Quebec and Winnipeg moved to Colorado and Phoenix, it was a tremendous loss.

And when you look at where the NHL put expansion teams in the U.S. — the non-hockey markets like Florida and Nashville where the teams are having trouble staying afloat — it was done in the name of television and marketing, and I think it was an error. In the U.S., hockey is a regional sport, and as David Hill, the president of Fox Sports, said, "What you want is strong regions." People in Detroit want to see the Red Wings. People in Boston want to see the Bruins. That's just the way it is. Regional ratings have always remained good — and in some areas, they're very strong.

And look at the labour problems under Bettman. There was a referees' strike in 2001, a 104-day lockout of the players in 1994 and a lockout that cost the entire 2004–05 season. In 1994, Bettman signed a one-sided agreement that gave most of the power to NHLPA boss Bob Goodenow and the players, and then he renewed it! Bettman got major television deals in the United States with Fox and ESPN, then lost them. He left ESPN, the leading sports network in the world, and went to Versus, a network that many Americans can't get because it's only on digital cable — and those who do get it can't find it. ESPN and Fox did a great job with hockey. They also had strong sports programming to cross-promote the games.

Bettman charges the CBC $100 million to televise games in Canada, but he has a deal with NBC in the United States that is based on profit-sharing — NBC doesn't pay rights fees. My late boss, Ted Hough, would have loved to have had that deal.

Yes, he beat down the players in the 2004–05 lockout, but I find it hard to believe that the league had to shut down for an entire season for him to get what it wanted. I think the real goal was to crush Goodenow, which ultimately happened. The owners got the salary cap they wanted, but I am convinced that they could have done it without losing a full season. Remember co-operation, goodwill and collaboration? Whoops, that was in the Ziegler era.

Clarence Campbell always said that a lot of things in the NHL come from the bottom, but leadership comes from the top. To me, Bettman has not been a good leader.

Why? His major error was not paying any attention to the product. For years, when asked about the problems in the game, Bettman would smile and say things like, "The game is fine. We have a great game. We are moving forward."

That simply was not true. NHL hockey looked more like a rodeo, with hooking and holding hampering the game's most gifted players. That style of hockey filtered down into minor hockey, where the emphasis was taken off developing skill and shifted to *limiting* creativity. Superstars like Pittsburgh's Mario Lemieux repeatedly complained, in vain, about all the obstruction.

"Everything is fine," Bettman would say. "We have a great game."

Now he takes bows for something the players initiated. It was Shanahan and his committee that finally got the game steered in the right direction with their innovative ideas.

The last time I spoke with Bettman, I was in Calgary at meetings of the International Olympic Committee and staying at the Palliser Hotel. Little did I know that the NHL was holding its meetings there, too.

I went to the hotel bar, and there were a bunch of NHL guys, among them vice-president Colin Campbell, who invited me over for a drink. Who joins us out of the blue, but Gary Bettman. "Be careful, Ralph," I warned myself. "You were invited by league guys to join them. Watch what you say. You are their guest and you're out of the game."

Well, Bettman asked the magic question. And you have to remember, this was before the lockout of 2004–05, when the league was still all clutch-and-grab. The fans knew the hockey we were seeing was awful.

Bettman asked, "What do you think of our league now, Ralph?"

I couldn't believe he asked me that question. So I said to myself, "If he's asking the question, I'm going to tell him."

"It's worse than ever," I replied. "Too much expansion has watered down the league. Half the players in the league wouldn't have made it twenty years ago. The product is terrible. It's all clutch-and-grab, and the coaches are forced to go to the lowest common denominator — obstruction and holding and interference."

You should have seen his face. Very seldom do you see Gary Bettman speechless.

Colin Campbell really took me to task right away — thank heavens. I have a lot of respect for Colin.

"How dare you talk to our commissioner that way?" Campbell said.

"Look," I responded, "if I can talk to [IOC president] Juan Antonio Samaranch this way, I can certainly talk to Gary Bettman this way. Besides, he asked me the big question." I have strong feelings about people I feel have hurt our game, and I don't mind expressing them.

I got up and walked out. It upset me, because I had to leave a full rum and Coke behind. That's what really hurt — especially since the NHL was buying!

In fairness, though, let's see what the future holds for Bettman's regime. It's time to look ahead. The competition committee's new rules are working: the game is faster and the skilled players are now being allowed to give us great entertainment. I hope we can continue to move forward with additional new rules. Hey Gary, how about no-touch icing? How about changing only on the fly? And how about a serious penalty for headhunting? And why not eliminate fighting once and for all? It's time. The U.S. television guys would love it.

And then maybe, in a future edition, I can change the title of this segment to "The Revolution in the NHL: How Gary Bettman Saved Hockey." I hope so. Meanwhile, I hope I won't have to keep trying to find the Versus Network on my cable system for very much longer.

FINAL BUZZER
A FATHER
ON HIS SON

Chapter 22

THE HEART AND SOUL HOCKEY PLAYER
SCOTT MELLANBY

If I had been a betting man, I would have wagered that my son, Scott, would become a professional tennis player, golfer or baseball player before he would make it to the NHL.

Shows how much I know!

Born in Montreal but raised in Toronto, Scott was a fabulous athlete from a very young age, but although he had a passion for hockey, he was more accomplished in these other sports.

A point I like to get across when I talk to minor hockey groups or parents about my son is that I wanted him to play all kinds of sports, as I did when I was young. And, although my dad and all his uncles were great athletes, which might suggest it was a given that Scott would also be an elite athlete, I never had inflated expectations for him. The odds of making it to the NHL are too steep — only about one-half of 1 percent of all kids who play hockey actually make it to the NHL.

We told our kids — Scott and his sister, Laura — that no matter what they do in life, whether they are a plumber or a garbage collector, they only have to give it their all and be the best. My hopes for Scott were that he would have a good and happy life and, if he played sports, to enjoy them. Here, for all you hockey mothers and fathers, is his story — a story about hockey and a dream come true.

Because I was a professional baseball player and knew how difficult it can be, I was able to help Scott keep his feet on the ground. At the ages of seven and eight he played baseball, golf, tennis and badminton. However, he kept begging me to put him on an elite hockey team.

"No," I would tell him. "Just go out with your friends and have fun at the local rink."

We lived near the Kingsway in Toronto, and nearby was the Humber Valley Arena, where there was an outdoor artificial rink where the kids could play shinny. So that's what Scott would do — he would play shinny for hours on end, just like kids did in the old days.

Finally, when Scott was eight, I gave in and let him play organized hockey. I had said that I didn't want him enrolled in organized sports until he was ten, but his grandfather — Janet's dad — said, "This kid is good, Ralph. He should be playing on a team." For a change, I listened. I put him in the Humber Valley House League with all his pals, and his coach, Ron Connal, was great. All he would tell the kids was, "Go out and have a lot of fun ... and score goals." I wouldn't have wanted to be the goalie on that team.

In any case, they won the championship, so it turned out to be a great start for Scott. He wasn't the highest scorer or the best player by any stretch of the imagination, but he was playing with his friends and he really enjoyed that first year.

In the meantime, he was still playing baseball in the summer, as well as golf and tennis down at Toronto's Boulevard Club. It was a good time in life for him; a real time of pure innocence and great fun.

Of all the sports he played, hockey was probably his weakest. He went to the Ontario Under-12 final in tennis (losing to Andrew Sznajder, who later became a top Canadian pro), and he was a great baseball player, the best player on his team when he was ten and eleven. He beat me at golf when he was twelve years old — although, as Bobby Orr once said, "That's not a giant accomplishment."

But Scott loved hockey so much that he used to say to me, "Dad, winter is coming. I can smell the ice!"

For years I sent him to Howie Meeker's Hockey School, which is interesting in itself. Howie told me that, of the thousand of kids who attended his hockey schools over the years, Scott was the only one to make it to the NHL. Imagine that! He repaid Howie by going to his hockey school in 1987, after he played in the Stanley Cup finals with the Philadelphia Flyers, and working without a fee as a guest instructor.

Many fathers seem to have such high expectations for their boys in hockey. Not me. I was a realist. Scott was a second-liner, especially when he got to Triple-A in Mississauga. I let him play at that level when he was twelve because I thought it would be nice if he got the opportunity to go to the big annual peewee tournament in Quebec City, which he did. Many great NHLers say that playing in the Quebec Peewee Tournament was one of their greatest thrills. Scott scored the first goal of the tournament, and then didn't score again.

Scott wasn't a natural scorer. Nor could he fall back on size: he was very small and very skinny, which really used to bug him. I was six foot one and his mom was five foot ten.

It would drive him to tears. "When am I going to grow?" he would ask his mother plaintively.

And Janet would say, "Don't worry, your time will come."

While he was still with Mississauga, the coach of his rep team quit and the new coach benched him. There he was, thirteen years old, riding the pine. I thought it was ridiculous, so I took him out of the rep program and put him back in house league for a year.

Scott, naturally, was devastated, although I was convinced I was doing it for his own good. What's the point of playing rep hockey if you're going to sit on the bench? You want to play hockey when you are a kid. Benching kids is ridiculous.

The following season he tried out for the Toronto Marlboros, midgets. It was weird back then. Because he'd sat out a year of rep hockey, he was a free agent and could try out for whichever team in Toronto he chose. If he hadn't sat out the year, he would have remained the property of Mississauga. It's a terrible system.

Scott was the last cut with the Marlies, but he had also gone to one practice with the Don Mills Flyers, so when he was released we hustled him into the car and drove across town, and he tried out for — and made — the Flyers. That was the year he finally had a growth spurt. He sprouted up a few inches and added some muscle. He also benefited from great coaches — John Edgar and Ed Robichaud — at Don Mills.

Scott played two years with the Flyers, going to the national championship tournament in the second season, and he played very well, but again, he wasn't a first-line player. He played on the third line with Mike Richard (who wound up playing seven games in the NHL with the Washington Capitals before playing fourteen years professionally in Switzerland). Future NHLers Peter Zezel and Kirk McLean also played on those teams.

I only took Scott to two NHL games a year when he was a kid. I didn't want him to feel like he was somebody special because of his dad's job. However, in 1980, I brought Scott — who was then thirteen years old — to the Stanley Cup finals between the New York Islanders and Philadelphia Flyers. We travelled between Philly and Long Island by bus. He had the time of his life.

He brought his skates and sweats, and because Bobby Clarke and I were close, I arranged for Scott to skate with the Flyers during an optional practice at the Spectrum. He actually looked pretty good out there, and the funny thing was that he was wearing his Don Mills Flyers tracksuit, which had the same colours and logo as the Philadelphia Flyers.

My friend Ed Snider, who owned the Flyers, was standing beside me and said, "Who's that kid out there? He's good."

"That's my boy," I said proudly.

Scott came over to the bench at one point and looked up into the Spectrum and said to his mom, "Someday I'm going to play here."

I laughed and said something to the effect of, "Don't get too carried away."

Well, his mother got mad and scolded me. "Don't kill his dream," Janet said to me. "Let him dream. If he makes it, great. If he doesn't, that's another matter."

I learned a lesson that day: let your children dream and keep encouraging them.

As Scott continued in hockey, I felt that if he could make the Henry Carr Crusaders, one of the better Junior B teams in Metropolitan Toronto, he would be eligible for a scholarship to an American university and might one day play for the Canadian Olympic team. I still had no vision of Scott playing in the NHL.

The Crusaders, who were associated with Father Henry Carr High School in Etobicoke, had won the provincial Junior B championship the season before Scott joined them, and their graduates included Bob Essensa, Patrick Flatley and the Cavallini brothers, Gino and Paul, all of whom went on to have successful NHL careers after college. Everything the Crusaders did was based on their kids eventually advancing to college hockey. They practised five days a week and played twice a week.

I had lunch with the team's coaches, Peter Miller and Dan Cameron, and was told in no uncertain terms that Scott would have to try out for the team and make it on his own terms. It didn't matter to them who the kid was or what level he had played at previously, he had to earn a spot on the team. That was the rule.

I didn't go to the first tryouts, and when Scott came home, he was surprised at how he he'd been treated in practice. I guess they wanted to see how tough, physically and mentally, Scott was. They charged him and rammed him and hacked him to see how much he could take.

"They really tested me," he told me. "But I'm standing up to them."

When I finally went to a practice, I asked Cameron, "Is Scott going to make the team?"

The answer I received floored me.

"He's not only going to make the team, he's going to be a first-round draft choice in the NHL!" Cameron said.

Scott really blossomed playing Junior B — he scored a pile of goals (37 in 39 games) and led the league in points (with 74). And he finally became a first-line player. Teams from the Ontario Hockey League began scouting him. We also had recruiters from U.S. colleges visiting our home, hoping to convince Scott that their program was the best one for him. Of the thirty-two teams in Division I of the NCAA, Scott spoke with thirty-one. Lots of coffee and doughnuts were served in our recreation room that year!

I would have preferred that Scott choose the college route, rather than play major junior, but I wanted him to make his own decision. Still, I had my friend Sherry Bassin, the loquacious general manager of the Oshawa Generals, make a pitch about why college hockey wouldn't be the right path for a player who wanted to make it to the NHL. Sherry assured us that he would draft Scott if he decided to go the junior route.

After Sherry left, Scott remarked, "Boy, that guy can sure talk."

An old friend of mine, Fred Sorel, wound up drafting Scott to play major junior for his Windsor Spitfires. Fred called me, and I asked him why the heck he would draft Scott. He said, "Well, with you being from Windsor, I thought you might talk him into playing here."

"I spent my whole life getting out of Windsor!" I replied. "Fred, I love you, but you just wasted your first-round pick."

Scott was also taken in the NHL entry draft that season, although it turned out that Cameron was just a little bit optimistic: he was chosen in the *second* round, twenty-seventh overall. Which, in today's thirty-team NHL, would make him a first-rounder. But it is extremely rare for a player to be drafted out of Junior B (especially when he's headed for college), and Scott was picked ahead of such future superstars as Patrick Roy, Luc Robitaille and Brett Hull. Obviously, NHL scouts saw great potential in Scott. And the team that drafted him? The Philadelphia Flyers.

Ultimately, Scott opted to go to college on a scholarship. He was very interested in studying business, so he visited Michigan State, the University of New Hampshire and the University of Wisconsin. Michigan and New Hampshire were fine, but at Wisconsin hockey was the number one sport — all others were secondary. I was also aware of UW's fine reputation for academics. Scott was recruited by their longtime coach, the legendary "Badger" Bob Johnson, who was coaching the Calgary Flames at the time, as well as former Badger and Henry Carr Crusader Patrick Flatley.

Scott really enjoyed his two years with the Badgers; he scored 14 goals and 38 points in 40 games in his first season and 21 goals and 44 points in 32 games in his second. Wisconsin had a very good team that featured a number of future NHLers, including Tony Granato, Gary Suter, Paul Ranheim, David Maley and goalie Mike Richter. Jeff Sauer was the coach — a great one.

I was shooting a series, *Baseball Pro Tips*, in Florida with Duke Snider and Tony Kubek when, out of the blue, Scott showed up after the 1985–86 season. I didn't know it at the time, but Scott and his mom had a plan up their sleeves.

At first, they told me he just wanted to drop by and say hello, but then he blurted out the truth: "Bobby Clarke wants me to sign with the Flyers now, just to be around the team at the end of the season. He wants me to see what NHL life is like and get to know the guys for the future."

There was no way I wanted him to leave Wisconsin early just to end up playing in the minors, so I negotiated his contract for him. I got a large signing bonus, but the sticking point in negotiations was the fact I wanted him on a one-way contract (that is, one that paid the same salary whether he was with the Flyers or not). Clarke told me that no Flyer rookie had ever been given a one-way deal, including himself. Besides, he said, coach Mike Keenan — "Iron Mike" — would hate it.

"Well, then," I said, "you are going to make Flyers history. Because the only way Scott will sign is if he gets a one-way deal. That's final."

I didn't think another year in school would hurt Scott, and if he did that, he could play in 1987–88 for the Canadian Olympic team under coach Dave King. King had told me that Scott would make the team. Remember, I was also living in Calgary, as I was handling the television duties for the 1988 Winter Games.

When I told Clarke over the phone that Scott wouldn't sign and perhaps we'd get a deal done next year, Scott was sitting there on the bed in my hotel room in West Palm Beach. When he heard this, he was decimated (remember the dream?).

"Don't worry," I told Scott, who was only nineteen at the time. "He'll call back." I also told him I thought it would be best if he played another year at Wisconsin and then played in the Olympics.

"Look what happened to you, Dad," he said. "You tore up your leg and never made it to the big leagues. I don't want to go back. What if I bust up my knee like you did? My dream would be over."

He added, "Let me play, and when my career is over, I'll go back to school and get my degree."

Sure enough, Clarke called back within the hour and said, "You have your deal."

And Scott played twenty-one years in the NHL and made millions. I don't think he'll need to go back to Wisconsin.

The Flyers used him in only two regular-season games in what was left of 1985–86, but he learned about the NHL. And about life. He was invited out for a beer with a few of the veterans (Dave Poulin, Tim Kerr and Mark Howe), and he was all geared up to live the lifestyle of a young NHLer — or at least his concept of it: beautiful women, lots of fanfare and lots of laughs. Was he ever disappointed ... all they talked about was money!

"Who's your financial advisor? Who's your broker? How much of a signing bonus did you get?"

Later, he told me, "All these guys are interested in is investments and business. And they only had one beer each, then they left for home!"

His mom and I went to his first home game the next season. Early in the game, Scott made a mistake that cost the Flyers a goal. Of course, the people behind us didn't know who we were, and they got all over Scott, the Flyers' only rookie.

"Who the hell is this kid?"

"He's awful!"

At the end of the period, Janet and I stood up and the folks behind us asked, "Where are you from?"

"Calgary."

"What brings you here?"

"My son is Number 19, Scott Mellanby." They were astonished and speechless.

You should have heard them the next period. Scott scored his first goal, a beauty, and the guys behind us really started talking him up. They became the unofficial Scott Mellanby Fan Club for many years.

Early in his career, Scott was Mike Keenan's whipping boy, probably because of his one-way contract. Keenan loved to hold the fact that he could send kids to the minors over their heads — it was his way of controlling them.

I still run into former teammates of Scott's who tell me that they don't know how he survived Keenan. Keenan was on Scott every day. He'd walk into the dressing room and say things like, "Who is the only player in here with a silver spoon in his mouth?" That was obviously a reference to Scott's contract.

Years later, Keenan, who was with Chicago at the time, asked me out to dinner. I was in the Tri-Cities region of Washington State, televising the Goodwill Games, and all the NHL scouts and GMs were there in the desert to scout the national teams.

Mike and I had a few "pops," and suddenly he said, "You know, Ralph, I've matured a lot since I coached Scott, and he has matured a lot, too. I'm going to trade for him. He's going to become a Blackhawk."

Scott had always played well in Chicago — he always scored a goal and got into a fight — so I wasn't surprised that Mike would be interested in obtaining him.

I sat there quietly for a few seconds, then I looked him right in the eye and said, "Mike, he hates your guts!"

Mike leaned back in his chair and said, "Yeah, you're right. He hates my guts. No trade."

I told Scott about the conversation and he laughed. "Dad, you did me a great favour."

That said, Scott values the time he played for Keenan.

"Dad, I was a kid who had stars in my eyes and his treatment made me as hard as steel," Scott said.

I thought Scott would be a Flyer for life, but Bobby Clarke was fired and the guy who replaced him, Russ Farwell, traded him to Edmonton for Jari Kurri, a Hall of Famer, in May of 1991. Hey, if Wayne Gretzky can be traded, I guess anybody is fair game. To this day, I run into fans from Philadelphia who say that trading Scott — and Rick Tocchet a year later — were the worst trades the Flyers ever made.

Scott played two years in Edmonton with the Oilers, eight with the Florida Panthers, four with the St. Louis Blues and his final two seasons with the Atlanta Thrashers — twenty-one years in total. He also played in the 1996 NHL All-Star Game in Boston.

(At this point, I must also mention that my beautiful daughter, Laura, who also went to Wisconsin, became a fine television producer, was a vice-president at CTV and Sportsnet, VP of programming at ESPN Asia in Singapore and is now Director, Pay-per-View, for Bell Globemedia in Canada. I always said that Laura and Scott got their mom's looks ... *and* their talent. She and Scott are my superstars.)

The family is deeply proud of the fact that Scott was captain of both the Panthers and the Thrashers. In fact, when Scott retired after the 2006–07 season, his coach, Bob Hartley, said, "He has helped show our younger players what it means to be a professional and how to represent an organization with class."

One of the most memorable moments in Scott's career came on opening day of the 1995–96 season, when he killed a rat inside the Panthers' dressing room in the morning and then went out and scored two goals that night. Goalie John Vanbiesbrouck said Scott scored a "rat trick." Fans jumped all over that, and by the end of the year they were littering the ice with plastic rats every time Florida scored. The Panthers, in just their third year of operation, shocked the hockey world by making it to the Stanley Cup finals, only to lose to the Colorado Avalanche.

Scott completed his NHL career having played 1,431 games. He was known as a grinder, but he had pretty good hands, too, and finished with 364 goals, 476 assists and 840 points. Never one to turn the other cheek, he also accumulated 2,479 penalty minutes.

I should tell you that, when Scott started his career, my friend Don Cherry was visiting and took Scott out into our backyard to teach him how to fight. Scott didn't always win during his NHL career, but he didn't lose too many, either — thanks, Grapes!

As I look back, it's funny. I never criticized Scott for his play on the ice. He played with Canada's team at the World Junior Championship, he played in the National Midget Championships, the Peewee Tournament in Quebec and the Stanley Cup finals — twice. To this day, he will tell you, "According to my dad, I have never played a bad game of hockey."

I always followed the philosophy that you should pick out the positives and dwell on the good plays, not the mistakes. Toe Blake, the Hall of Fame coach, once told me: "Hockey is a game of repetition — and mistakes. You do the same thing over and over again until someone makes a mistake. And someone always will."

Father David Bauer, my friend and a Hall of Fame coach and priest, always said, "With your players, always dwell on the positive."

Howie Meeker added: "Hockey is fun for kids, not an ego trip for parents. Most parents should be barred from the arena."

I am so proud of Scott and his hockey career, and equally proud of him as a man, a father and a husband. Frank Selke once told me that he never met anyone in the NHL who didn't have great respect and admiration for my boy. I am very proud to know that, and respect him as much as a man as I do as a hockey player.

Glen Sather said it all, I think: "Scott is the boy every man dreams of having." I am lucky I had him, and I am honoured to include him in this book. To me, he is a legend, and I love him.

INDEX

231

Index

Index